Ethics of Biblical Interpretation

Ethics of Biblical Interpretation

A Reevaluation

DANIEL PATTE

Westminster John Knox Press
Louisville, Kentucky

Book and cover design by Drew Stevens

First edition

Published by Westminster John Knox Press
Louisville, Kentucky

This book is printed on acid-free paper that meets the American National Standards Institute Z39.48 standard. ∞

PRINTED IN THE UNITED STATES OF AMERICA

95 96 97 98 99 00 01 02 03 04 — 10 9 8 7 6 5 4 3 2 1

Library of Congress Cataloging-in-Publication Data
Patte, Daniel, date.
    Ethics of biblical interpretation : a reevaluation / Daniel Patte.
  —1st ed.
        p.   cm.
    Includes bibliographical references.
    ISBN 0-664-25568-X (alk. paper)
    1. Bible—Hermeneutics. 2. Hermeneutics—Moral and ethical aspects. 3. Christian ethics. I. Title.
BS476.P328   1995
220.6'01—dc20   94-47641

To Gary Phillips

Contents

Acknowledgments

Acknowledgments are here most appropriate because the quest that this book represents could not have progressed without the help and support of many. It was not easy to reevaluate my exegetical practices and to discover that through them I had hurt other people instead of helping them. At first, I resisted these conclusions. I refused to acknowledge that the problem was directly related to the one-dimensional character of my exegeses and to the implicit and arrogant universal claims that dismiss as worthless any and all ordinary readings.

I would still resist these conclusions, if it were not for, first, the amazingly gentle (although at times not so gentle) prodding of many people, including many students whom I hurt with my exegetical practices and, second, for the critical analyses of our practices as male European-American exegetes that feminist, African-American, and other advocacy scholars had the patience to provide for us. I acknowledge their many contributions to these reflections in the following pages. Here it is enough to gratefully acknowledge those who facilitated these transforming encounters: Dr. Craig Dykstra and the Lilly Endowment for a grant in support of a conference on Ethical Responsibilities and Practices in Biblical Criticism, held at Vanderbilt University, in March 1991, which revealed to me what is involved in the decentering of male European-American critical exegetical practices; and Dean Bernard Lategan, Stellenbosch University, and the Human Science Research Council of South Africa for a grant in support of a visit in South Africa, which helped me recognize the central and primary place of ordinary readings in any critical interpretation.

It was not enough, however, to shift perspective and to reach new conclusions regarding appropriate exegetical practices. I needed to let go of my androcentric and Eurocentric ways of envisioning myself and my task as a critical exegete. I needed to undergo a paradigm shift that allowed me spontaneously to view the critical exegetical task as *the bringing to critical understanding of a faith-interpretation*, so much so that decentered exegetical and pedagogical practices would become "natural" for me. I still have a long way to go to reach this goal. But I had the confidence to progress toward this goal because of the support of certain friends and colleagues. I welcomed their often severe criticism of my work and practice because their comments also were an expression of confidence in the ultimate value of my quest.

Although I am sure they will have new criticisms for the present form of my proposal, I have to acknowledge the special contributions to this book of five of my friends/colleagues. Peter Paris's criticism of a key feature of an earlier version of this book (a feature presented in an article published in collaboration with Gary Phillips) helped me at last to recognize and accept the necessary ambivalence of my proposal and stance. Fred Burnett, Timothy Cargal, Gary Phillips, and Larry Welborn had similar roles. In an intense and most extraordinary three-day session in 1989, they shredded the very first version of this book; the shifting of paradigm had begun, so much so that we were "chasing wild boars" (Burnett's appropriate description). Yet because of their support, I was quickly back at work on a totally different second version of this book. Our joint concerns about ethics of biblical interpretation were also formulated in the form of a proposal for the 1991 Vanderbilt conference, coauthored with Gary Phillips. This formulation was, in turn, thoroughly revised in response to our feminist, African-American, and Hispanic-American colleagues at that conference. Once again, I had to throw away a draft of this book.

Without the ongoing support of Burnett, Cargal, and Phillips, the confusion of undergoing this paradigm shift would have been paralyzing rather than constructive. Fred Burnett's insightful analyses and humor gave me the confidence to step into the unknown of a decentered world. Gary Phillips as the codirector of the project played an essential role. Together, through electronic mail as well as in person, we unpacked the many facets of the conference discussions and coauthored a detailed report and an article. This extraordinary collaboration, such that it soon became impossible to distinguish the origin of ideas in one or the other of us, gave me the confidence to progress in this decentering venture by writing a new version of this book.

The style and content of the third version were greatly refined by Nicole Wilkinson's trusted editing and suggestions, by Betsy Cagle's word processing, and by Nancy Roseberry's copyediting. I am most grateful to each of them. Yet it is to Gary Phillips that I owe the greatest debt of gratitude. We have so much "thought together" (often, in cyberspace!) about these issues that I am totally unable to say which are the points in this book that were first suggested by him. I know that he certainly will have many criticisms of this final form of the book, since my rewriting of significant parts of the third version in light of his comments could not take into account all his critical observations on it (more than twenty single-spaced pages!). But I also know that much of this book comes from him, because it was written in constant dialogue with him. It is written to Gary Phillips.

Introduction: Adopting an Androcritical Perspective

This book on ethics of biblical interpretation is deliberately ambivalent. It reflects tensions within my own thinking that are rooted both in who I am and in the pluralistic and global context in which I strive to practice biblical critical studies, through teaching and research. The designation "post-modern" might be an appropriate way to express my ambivalence; this term conveys that I am *both* "modern" *and* "something else," since a post-modern perspective is necessarily the modification of a modern one.

I am a critical exegete, committed to the production of critical readings of the Bible, that is, readings that establish and verify their own legitimacy through the use of critical methods, themselves based upon critical (scientific) theories. I am "modern."

Yet I am conscious of the fact that my interpretations, including my critical readings, reflect and are marked by the perspective from which I interpret. For instance, since I am a male raised and educated in Europe and North America, my interpretations are *either* "androcentric" and "Eurocentric" (terms I use for designating interpretations by male "European-Americans"[1] who *are not* self-conscious about the contextual character of their interpretations) *or* "androcritical" (a term I use for designating interpretations by male European-Americans who *are* self-conscious about the contextual character of their interpretations). I am "post-modern."

My ambivalence is reflected in many other tensions that I shall make as explicit as possible throughout this book. The tension between responsibility and accountability needs to be clarified at the outset, since it concerns the very conception of "ethics of biblical interpretation." On the one hand, I want to underscore that we, male European-American critical exegetes, *must assume responsibility* for the effect of our work upon various groups of people, especially when this effect is quite negative. In this latter case, we must of course look for ways to correct this situation. Yet, the moral obligation to assume responsibility for our critical exegeses is not without its own ambivalence. It involves adopting a view of ethics according to which critical biblical interpretation and ethics, as well as critical scholars and ordinary readers, are in a hierarchical relationship, which already establishes a structure of oppression and injustice. This structure can remain uncontested because in this perspective ethics is viewed as an add-on, or even as an afterthought, rather than as an intrinsic and structuring aspect of critical exegetical practices.

On the other hand, when I take into account the contextual character of my own perspective—an "androcritical perspective"—I have to conclude that *ethical accountability* in critical exegesis is possible only insofar as we view our critical exegetical task as a practice that is fundamentally conceived and framed in terms of the ethical. Critical interpretation is a praxis that is intrinsically ethical, because from its starting point to its concluding point it is structured by concerns for others (and the Other). Consequently, as I discuss below, the otherness of ordinary readers and of their interpretations is not viewed as opposed to critical readings, and the relationship between critical and ordinary readers is no longer hierarchical. In brief, it is only when critical exegesis is conceived as a practice of ethics that it can be ethically accountable.

Then, should I reject the former conception of an ethics of critical reading, an ethics of responsibility, so as to keep only the latter, an ethics of accountability? Of course not! The tension between these two views of ethics of biblical interpretation must remain. Both perspectives are necessary. Without the former conception, we cannot truly assume responsibility for the effects of our critical interpretations, and thus we cannot envision the urgent need of ethically responsible exegetical practices. Without the latter conception, we cannot hope to develop ethically accountable exegetical practices (the need for which we envisioned because of the former conception). Conversely, even if we develop ethically accountable exegetical practices according to the latter conception, it is to be expected that, because of our sinful nature,[2] we will at times (to say the least) fail to be ethically responsible in our critical exegetical practices. But, in order to perceive these failures, we need to assume responsibility for our critical exegeses and its effects upon people, something that requires the former conception of ethics—the weakness of the ethics of accountability is that it does not provide the "objective" critical perspective that allows us to hold ourselves responsible for the negative effects of our critical practices. In sum, both conceptions of ethics of biblical interpretation are imperfect. But both are necessary, because each has a positive contribution to make.

A discussion of these two conceptions of ethics of biblical interpretation and of the tension that I propose to maintain between them offers a first glance at the way in which this book unfolds.

Assuming Responsibility for Our Critical Exegeses

Are we ethically responsible when we perform critical exegesis? When we present in writing the results of our critical studies to an indefinite public of potential readers? When we teach critical biblical studies to classes in an academic or a church context? When we preach on the basis of a critical exegetical study of a biblical text?

Such are the questions with which I began the writing of this book. As I formulated these questions, I was quite aware that a few years earlier it would not have occurred to me to raise them. I recognized that I benefited from an exceptional conjunction of learning experiences that drastically changed my outlook and progressively led me to raise ethical questions concerning my practices as a critical exegete. I was also aware that without this change of outlook, I would not have discovered that my answer to each of these questions had to be a resounding "No, we are not ethically responsible" (when "we" is defined as "male European-American critical exegetes," as it is throughout this book unless otherwise noted). Consequently, one of my main goals in this book is to help my colleagues raise the issues of our ethical responsibility as critical exegetes, insofar as they are not yet doing so. (Those whom I designate as "my colleagues" are the very diverse practitioners of critical biblical studies in academic and church circles, and especially male European-American critical exegetes.)

Toward this goal, I must first convince others of the need for a change of outlook—a paradigm shift—similar to the one I have undergone. For this purpose, as I discuss herein, a theoretical or methodological argument will be ineffective. Since my outlook was transformed by concrete experiences, and not by arguments, the best I can do is to describe my own experiences and the ways in which they transformed my perspective regarding critical biblical studies. My hope is that my colleagues will be able to identify with what has happened to me and to recognize that they are faced with these same ethical issues, even if they have not been as directly confronted by them as I have. In sum, we have to acknowledge that, despite all our good intentions, we fail to be ethically responsible so long as we practice critical biblical exegesis in a traditional manner.

When I had clarified for myself this failure to be ethically responsible, I thought that the rest of the book could then unfold in clearly marked steps: (1) a critical analysis of the causes of this ethically problematic critical practice and (2) a formulation of alternate ways of practicing critical biblical exegesis that, this time, would truly be ethically responsible. I envisioned that in its conclusions this book would devise a new methodology or a new procedure for ethically responsible critical biblical studies, which would then be illustrated by a concrete example.

This was a well laid-out plan. Indeed, it was the only one I could imagine, because I have been trained to proceed in a scientific and critical/methodological way: identify a problem; analyze it; formulate a way of addressing it; propose the solution. I could not be myself—that is, I could not be a "critical" exegete—if I did not proceed in this way. Thus, this book follows the above plan. Yet it does so only up to a point. Actually, its conclusions are not at all what I expected. This book does *not* conclude by presenting a new methodology or a new procedure for ethically responsible critical biblical studies. And this is as it should be.

What happened? In the very process of seeking to clarify why we male European-American critical exegetes fail to be ethically responsible in our critical practices, I recognized that, in a sense, this ethical problem is exemplified by the very procedure that I envisioned following in this book. Then, is not the solution obvious? Since the procedure proposed for this book is a part of the problem, should I not *abandon* it and *adopt another one*—one that would be truly ethically responsible? As I explain in chapter 1, this is what I tried to do several times. But despite radical changes in procedures, each time I ended up with the same problem, because the ethical problem does not ultimately reside in one perspective or another, but in the effort of having a single, nonambivalent, coherent view of "ethics of biblical interpretation." This universalizing (absolutizing) gesture unduly excludes other possible views, as if the preferred view of ethics did not itself reflect the limitations of its own contextual perspective. Even if it is well intentioned, such an exclusion of other people's views simply because they are different is a way of thinking that already conforms to oppression, such as racism or apartheid. The only way to proceed is thus to affirm the legitimacy of several different approaches, while recognizing the limitations of each.

The Ongoing Process of
Becoming Ethically Accountable

These observations suggest that I progressively discovered that ethical accountability in critical exegesis is an ongoing process, which demands that we constantly pass from one perspective to another, from one set of conclusions regarding the way to practice critical exegesis to another. Stopping this process at any point amounts to absolutizing and universalizing a specific contextual perspective, a step that leads to ethically problematic practices (see chapter 1). Consequently, I had to make sure that this book on ethics of biblical interpretation would not itself be ethically problematic by stopping the process, for instance, by proposing conclusions that would be a closure because they would offer "*the* ethical way of practicing critical exegesis"—a recipe, a procedure, a method. But how could I write such a book?

It turned out to be easier than I imagined. I discovered that it was simply a matter of presenting not merely the conclusions that I had reached regarding the issue of ethics of biblical interpretation but also the process through which I went as I progressively envisioned these conclusions in the course of preparing, writing, and editing this book, and then finally looking back at it. At each stage, I reached definite and unequivocal conclusions regarding the nature of the ethical problem we have to address and regarding ways of transforming our critical exegetical practices to make them ethically accountable. I soon discovered that these conclusions were not as unequivocal as I thought. While addressing one ethical problem, each solution had the potential to become part of the problem by engendering another kind of ethically problematic practice. Thus, I had to envision the ethical issue from another perspective, which in turn seemed initially definite and unequivocal, and so it went. In sum, each chapter of this book, while proposing significant conclusions that need to be incorporated into our practices of critical exegesis, also acknowledges the ambivalence of its conclusions. This acknowledgment requires that I consider the issue of ethical accountability in biblical interpretation from another perspective. This consideration becomes the topic of the next chapter, which proposes ambivalent conclusions. And so on, until the last chapter, which is not called "conclusions" because its results are themselves ambivalent; they call for looking at the reconceived practice of critical exegesis from a very different perspective, namely, the one from which we started.

Thus, if one wants to speak about the point (singular) that this book makes, one would have to say: Critical exegetical practices have the potential of being ethically accountable to their various constituencies only insofar as they constantly acknowledge the ambivalence of their procedures and thus affirm the need both to continue to follow these procedures and to practice exegesis according to very different procedures. This point—or better, this series of points and the process that engenders them—needs to be clarified by a general presentation of the forthcoming chapters.

A First View of the Ethical Problem:
Repenting from Our Sins[3]

As I first thought about the issue of ethics of biblical interpretation, the primary question was for me, Are we ethically responsible when we perform critical exegesis? This question is appropriate. As soon as this question is raised, it becomes clear that our traditional critical exegetical practices, while striving to satisfy the ethical demands of the Academy, fail to be accountable to many of those who are directly or indirectly affected by our interpretations, namely, ordinary readers of the Bible.

By raising this question, chapter 1 follows the suggestions made by Elisabeth Schüssler Fiorenza in her Society of Biblical Literature presidential address:[4] as male European-American critical exegetes, we have to acknowledge our failure to be accountable to the many readers of the Bible, including women, whom we have marginalized through our very practices of critical exegeses, and we must strive to find a way to correct this problem. By making the question of our ethical responsibility both to the Academy and to those affected by our work the topic of this chapter, I have adopted Schüssler Fiorenza's implicit definition of ethics, which finds expression in her presentation of the relationship between critical exegesis and ethics. She distinguishes between an "ethics of historical reading" (which I take to include all kinds of critical methodological approaches) and an "ethics of accountability" (which accounts "not only for the choice of theoretical interpretive models but also for the ethical consequences of the biblical text and its meanings").[5]

In chapter 1, by emphasizing the importance of the "ethics of accountability" as Schüssler Fiorenza suggests, I expose our lack of ethical accountability as male European-American critical exegetes. To put it bluntly, by systematically rejecting any interpretation that does not conform to our (male European-American) critical readings, we are sexist, racist, classist, colonialist—proponents of oppression in all its forms. This painful acknowledgment has been and still is for me an inescapable call to repentance. Practicing critical exegesis as usual became impossible. How could I continue a practice whose results were in direct contradiction with my deepest sense of vocation as a critical exegete?

Because I feel, with many other exegetes, that our vocation as *critical* exegetes is fundamentally valuable, I do not take this call to repentance to be a call to abandon our critical task. With Schüssler Fiorenza, I affirm the importance of holding together both an "ethics of critical reading" and an "ethics of accountability." From this perspective, one must acknowledge a problem with our traditional conception of "critical reading," because this conception causes us to lack accountability. The problem seems to be that we envision for each text the possibility of a single legitimate (i.e., critical) reading. The conflict between an ethics of critical reading and an ethics of accountability can be resolved if one conceives of a plurality of legitimate (critical) readings that is presented in the form of what I propose to call a "multidimensional critical exegesis."

Chapter 1 concludes with the suggestion that a multidimensional critical exegesis might be an ethically responsible practice, in the sense that it would satisfy both the ethics of critical reading and the ethics of accountability. These conclusions are nevertheless ambivalent and therefore include tensions that reveal their tentativeness. To begin with, there is the obvious question, Is it really plausible to envision a plurality of legitimate readings of a given text, with the understanding that some of these readings might be contradictory? This is the question I take up in chapter 2. Yet, in the proposed solution, there is another, more subtle tension that is already found in Schüssler Fiorenza's proposal.

The question is this: What is the relationship between "ethics of critical reading" and "ethics of accountability"? At this point in my reevaluation, I follow Schüssler Fiorenza; I presuppose that the issue of "critical reading" must be resolved before one can meaningfully raise the issue of accountability. Once the characteristics of "the biblical text and its meanings" have been satisfactorily established, the issue of ethical accountability can be raised about the results of this academic endeavor. The value of this academic investigation, with its choice of a theoretical interpretive model, is examined in terms of the way in which it ultimately affects other readers of the Bible: Is it or is it not a responsible critical study? The value of the biblical text and its meanings (as established by the critical investigation) is examined in terms of its ethical consequences for (accountability to) the wider public. This twin ethical questioning would, in Schüssler Fiorenza's proposal, *complement* the critical study. Thus, she writes:

> The careful reading of biblical texts and the appropriate reconstruction of their historical worlds and of their symbolic universes need to be complemented by a theological discussion of the contemporary religious functions of biblical texts which claim scriptural authority today in biblical communities of faith.[6]

Note that this view of the relationship between critical study and ethical accountability presupposes that critical exegesis is an undertaking prior to and distinct from the matter of ethical accountability, viewed as an evaluation of how people are affected by the results of the critical exegesis. The "ethics of critical reading" is a first-level evaluation; the "ethics of accountability" is a second-level evaluation, that is, an evaluation of the effects of verified critical readings.

These comments should not be taken to mean that the issues and the conclusions presented in chapter 1 are problematic or inappropriate. Looking back on our critical exegeses, we should—indeed, we must—raise the question of the way in which the wider public is affected by the biblical text and its meanings as we have critically established them. This is an essential part of our responsibility to this wider public. We must proceed to this evaluation of our work: It is an ethical imperative that we should not seek to escape. We must assume the responsibility for the negative effects upon many people whom our critical studies of the Bible marginalize(d) and help(ed) to oppress, however unintentionally. For this purpose, we must raise the question, "Are we ethically responsible, when we perform critical exegesis?" And then we must proceed to address the problem this question leads us to uncover.

I emphasized that we *must* assume responsibility for the effects of our work upon the wider public and that it is good to do so, because I now want to underscore that raising the question of our responsibility as critical exegetes to ordinary readers of the Bible might itself be an irresponsible critical practice. The question of our ethical responsibility and the procedures it engenders (analyzing the problem, envisioning an alternative, resolving the problem) are themselves ethically problematic precisely when we take them as a necessary means to address the ethical problems they uncover. In this case, we take as a universal the view of the relationship between critical exegesis and ethics that they include, even though this view directly reflects our point of view as male European-American critical exegetes—a view dependent on our traditional position of power. As I have noted, the perspective that we needed for recognizing our lack of ethical responsibility has ethical and contextual limitations that must be acknowledged: It includes a perception of ourselves, male European-American critical exegetes, as hierarchically superior to those whom we negatively affect by our work. Thus, I do not deny the legitimacy and value of raising the question of the ethical accountability of our critical practices; unless we raise this question, we cannot perceive the ethical problems that pervade our practices. But we must also recognize that in order to assume responsibility for the ethical problems resulting from our lack of accountability to those who are affected by our work, we need to envision critical exegetical practices from a radically different perspective.

The conclusions of chapter 1 cannot but manifest this ambivalence;

similar conclusions are also found in chapter 2, where the tensions generated by this ambivalence become more explicit.

A Quest for Accountability:
Multidimensional Exegetical Practices

Despite the ambivalence mentioned above, the conclusions of chapter 1, according to which an ethically responsible practice of critical exegesis must be multidimensional, remain legitimate. Consequently, for
me, envisioning the plausibility of a multidimensional critical exegesis
becomes a part of my ethical duty to transform our critical practices so
that they might truly be accountable to the many people who are directly or indirectly affected by our work. This is a quest for a methodological solution to the ethical problem; it seeks to envision the theory
about text and interpretation, itself based upon an appropriate epistemology, which provides the framework for conceiving of multidimensional critical procedures. This methodological quest took shape as
I struggled with the ethical problems—especially anti-Judaism and
patriarchalism—raised by a specific text, the Gospel according to
Matthew, and its interpretations. How could I, after Auschwitz, not
raise these issues?

For this purpose, in chapter 2 I argue that envisioning a text as se-
mantically multidimensional (textual polysemy) is at least as plausible
as traditional, one-dimensional views of text. Similarly, I argue for the
plausibility of acknowledging that any reading, including any critical
reading, is the production of meaning by the reader with one or another of the meaning-producing dimensions of the text, consciously or
subconsciously chosen because it matches the interests or concerns of
the reader. Finally, I argue for the plausibility of recognizing that the
diverse readings based upon different meaning-producing dimensions
of a text are equally legitimate because none of these dimensions can
be said to be a more legitimate representation of the meaning of the
text than the others.

In sum, chapter 2 seeks to establish the methodological basis for a
multidimensional critical exegetical practice, which would recognize
that various readings are equally legitimate, and thus would open the
possibility of acknowledging the legitimacy of very different readings
by groups with quite distinct contextual concerns and interests. Thus,
the suppression of feminist, African-American, and other advocacy
readings—the basic form that our lack of accountability to these
groups takes—could potentially be overcome.

Yet, the ambivalence that appeared at the end of chapter 1 pervades
chapter 2. Yes, it is a methodological quest. This methodological quest

is a necessary part of the process of discovering a practice of biblical interpretation that is both critical and accountable. But as I describe my own pilgrimage, I cannot but underscore issues of accountability even as I seek to argue points concerning critical readings. In practice, one cannot separate ethics of critical reading and ethics of accountability. Consequently, in chapter 2, I intermingle issues concerning both kinds of ethics. I do so certainly to the dismay both of those scholars primarily concerned with methods (traditionally, male European-American critical exegetes) and of those scholars primarily concerned with issues of accountability (most commonly, advocacy interpreters).

These tensions surface in the concluding section of chapter 2, where I describe two conceptions of multidimensional critical exegesis that are inappropriate because they do not foster ethical accountability to those who are affected by our exegetical work. In order to be ethically accountable, critical exegesis must be viewed as multidimensional. But this alone is *not sufficient*.

Critical Exegesis as an Intrinsically Ethical and Theological Practice

Chapter 3 describes the third step of my pilgrimage: the recognition that ethical responsibility in critical exegetical practice demands a different vision of the relationship between the critical readings and their ethical character, as well as between the critical readers and ethical readers. This became clear for me as I deliberately examined the interested nature of my own work as a critical exegete, thus adopting an androcritical perspective. I considered what one might want to call my "sense of vocation as a critical exegete." From this perspective, I first discovered that the lack of accountability to others inherent in our traditional critical exegetical practices was also and primarily a lack of accountability to ourselves: a fundamental betrayal of my vocation as a critical exegete, as well as a betrayal of my identity as a Protestant, and ultimately a betrayal of my ancestors, who died as martyrs rather than relinquish their freedom to read the Bible in their own ways. The line separating critical exegesis and ordinary (interested) readings was rapidly being erased.

In this light, critical exegeses was revealed to me in a new and exciting way. In brief, I discovered that any given critical exegesis is the bringing to critical understanding of an ordinary, interested reading. This formulation is voluntarily awkward so as to call to mind Anselm's *fides quaerens intellectum* (faith seeking understanding), and thus the recognition that critical exegesis is a theological practice that includes bringing to critical understanding *faith*-interpretations (among other ordinary readings). Then the reversal of the perception of the relationship between the ethical and the critical is complete. It is the ordinary reading that gives shape and value to the critical reading (not vice versa). Far from being primarily subjective (because interested) and thus illegitimate, all ordinary readings, which are authentic experiences of the text, should be viewed as reflecting actual meaning-producing dimensions of the text and thus as being basically legitimate.

From this perspective, the different readings proposed by ordinary readers should be welcomed and *affirmed* as legitimate by critical readers, whose task would be to discover the meaning-producing dimension of the text that is reflected by this reading. Similarly, and consequently, divergent critical readings should also be welcomed and affirmed as legitimate; indeed, they should be viewed as elucidating meaning-producing dimensions that were ignored in our own critical readings. Thus, our androcritical multidimensional exegetical practices should consist of recognizing and affirming the *otherness* of ordinary and critical readings by *other* people, as well as of recognizing and affirming the *otherness* of the text (as compared with the dimension of it that we had previously elucidated in our ordinary and critical readings).

The multidimensional androcritical exegetical task is then recognized not only as a theological one but also as an intrinsically *ethical* endeavor. From beginning to end it is fundamentally shaped by its encounter with the "other" (and the "Other"). While a clear distinction between the ethical and the critical questions can be maintained, they are now perceived as totally interdependent.

An Ethically Responsible Exegetical Practice
that Acknowledges Its Ambivalence

In chapter 4, I present systematically what currently should characterize the exegetical practice of male European-American exegetes if they are to be ethically responsible. In brief, it should be an *androcritical multidimensional exegetical practice*. Yet there is ambivalence in these conclusions, as there has been in each prior set of conclusions.

Here, the difficulty is that an androcritical multidimensional exegetical practice is totally devoted to affirming the legitimacy of any authentic reading, as well as valuing positively each of these readings as a disclosure of the "other." Consequently, from this standpoint, it becomes impossible to evaluate how our readings affect other people. Of course, theoretically, if it is truly androcritical, or, more generally, "other-oriented," our critical reading will not oppress other people or promote injustice. But as I have noted, it is essential to keep in mind our sinful human nature, and thus it is essential to examine the ways in which our critical readings affect others. For this, we need to come back to the beginning, raising again the questions raised in chapter 1.

Thus, my concluding paragraph sends us back to the beginning of the book so as to make clear that establishing an ethics of biblical interpretation is never achieved: It is a process, through which we must continuously examine and reexamine our interpretations and how they affect others. We have to assume responsibility for our critical work, even when it is androcritical and multidimensional.

The Form of My Argument

Many of my observations and proposals throughout this book are, to say the least, unexpected and surprising for most exegetes; some might call them fanciful or extravagant. This is so because these observations and proposals represent what one perceives when one looks at the phenomenon of "ethics of biblical interpretation" from different perspectives, or more precisely, from the perspectives of different paradigms.

Recognizing that there is an "ethical problem" in critical exegesis is possible for us only insofar as we undergo a paradigm shift, that is, a shift from one set of plausible presuppositions to another set of plausible presuppositions. Similarly, conceiving of the plausibility of multidimensional exegesis, as well as viewing critical exegesis as the bringing to critical understanding of an ordinary reading the otherness of which is affirmed, requires for most of us a paradigm shift. Consequently, one of my main goals is to facilitate this paradigm shift for the reader. For this purpose, my discourse needs to have a special form: a narrative, quasi-autobiographical form. Let me explain.

A paradigm shift is, in Schüssler Fiorenza's words, "an intellectual conversion [that] engenders a shift of commitment that allows the community of scholars to see old 'data' in a completely new perspective."[7] Only a new perspective puts us in a position truly to acknowledge *and to claim* what we are doing in our exegetical practices—pursuing concerns and interests of European-American males—and then to envision practices that will be ethically accountable, precisely because they keep the specificity of their goals (interests and concerns) in clear focus.[8]

Such a shift in paradigms, or intellectual conversion, simply "happens," rather than being decided or accepted because of the cogency of a well-developed argument. We shift paradigm when we can no longer resist the accumulated weight of basic questions that are raised by various, often apparently unrelated, aspects of our current perspective.[9] Then, in a long and continuing process, we have to assess the implications of this new perspective for all aspects of our work as critical exegetes. Thus, if I have personally shifted paradigm and if I can propose to my readers, especially to European-American male exegetes, that they undergo such a shift (if they have not done so yet), it is not because I have finished reassessing the implications of this shift for my critical exegetical practices, but rather because in the last twenty years or so, in our field and beyond, many such basic questions have been raised but not satisfactorily answered. Whether we have begun changing perspective or whether we resist doing so, the weight of these questions is upon us; and a paradigm shift is occurring all around us in the European-American culture in different guises (e.g., feminism, black theology, affirmation of minority rights, resistance to the "politically correct," calls for diversity in curriculum, globalization of theological education, methodological explosion).

Since it is the accumulated weight of these questions that may eventually bring about such a shift of paradigm, my task in this book is *not* to advocate such a shift through a cogent argument. It is simply to point out (1) the questions with which I struggled and that led me, a European-American male, to envision specific aspects of critical exegesis in a new perspective; (2) the ways in which these questions are traditionally addressed in the old paradigm; and (3) the ways in which these questions open up the possibility of envisioning critical exegetical practices in a new perspective. In sum, I simply seek to make explicit for male European-American exegetes the urgency and weight of these questions, with the hope of hastening the paradigm shift that is occurring for all of us whether we like it or not.

In order to make explicit the questions by which we are confronted, I tell the story of my resistance to this paradigm shift and how it won me over. For this, I proceed in a somewhat autobiographical way, which gives these chapters a narrative style. Conversions, intellectual or otherwise, whether they are called paradigm shifts, changes in perspective, or changes in presuppositions, are never easy. They happen only insofar as we can recognize in our own experiences—in our practices of critical exegesis—concrete problems that demand such a shift.

A Concluding Remark: The Place of
Ethical Theories in My Reflections

I self-consciously allowed the pragmatic dimensions of my experience as a male European-American critical exegete in a pluralistic world to structure my successive and diverse conceptualizations of the ethical problems and their envisioned solutions. Thus, I deliberately avoided basing my argument on theoretical considerations. Nevertheless, my reflections are informed by ethical theories. The plural *theories* is important. In keeping with the approach outlined above, I recognize and affirm the legitimacy of the three *distinct and divergent* branches of ethical theories, which Thomas W. Ogletree[10] calls consequentialist,[11] deontological,[12] and perfectionist[13] preunderstandings of the moral life.[14] This is so because my conception of ethics (of biblical interpretation) is primarily based upon the view that the ethical is fundamentally rooted in the affirmation of the otherness of the other (Other), as the essential move through which I define my self and my ethical responsibility.[15] In brief, for me, the acknowledgment and affirmation of the value of the otherness of the other is the foundation of ethics, precisely because it is "interested": it is only through my acknowledgment of the otherness of the other that I can acknowledge and affirm my own otherness and thus my own identity—my own self.[16] Conversely, the basic ethical problem in biblical interpretation occurs when we prevent others from affirming their own otherness, their own identity.

NOTES

1. "European-American" is used with a twofold meaning. In a narrow sense it refers to people from European origins living in North America (by contrast with African-Americans, Hispanic-Americans, etc.). In a broader sense, it also includes Europeans. Thus, it is shorthand for "persons of North Atlantic origins and cultures." The more precise compound term, "North Atlantic," is borrowed from Enrique Dussel, *Philosophy of Liberation* (Maryknoll, N.Y.: Orbis, 1985).

2. Note that according to the former conception of "ethics of biblical interpretation" (according to the "modern" perspective), one conceives of "universal" features, such as "sinful human nature" (although modern critical exegetes generally avoid talking about sin). One can also say that it is a rhetorical necessity to continue speaking from a "modern" perspective, because it is the only perspective from which the large majority of male European-American exegetes can envision the exegetical task. In order to be understood by my colleagues, I need to speak their "language." But, there is a more intrinsic reason; this is also "my language," the language through which I, a male European-American exegete, think and conceive of my task and of life.

3. Repentance from our lack of accountability as critical exegetes is emphasized both as a necessary first step in chapter 1 and also as an indispensable recurring step in chapter 4. Repentance thus provides a required framework for our ethics of interpretation, as Peter Paris, from whom I learned so much (see, in particular, his "The Bible and the Black Churches," in *The Bible and Social Reform*, ed. E. R. Sandeen [Philadelphia and Chico, Calif.: Fortress and Scholars, 1982], 133–54; and *The Social Teaching of the Black Churches* [Philadelphia: Fortress Press, 1985]), strongly emphasized in his detailed response to an article Gary Phillips and I published: "A Fundamental Condition for Ethical Accountability in the Teaching of the Bible by White Male Exegetes: Recovering and Claiming the Specificity

of Our Perspective," *Scriptura: Journal of Bible and Theology in Southern Africa*, S9 (1992) 7–28. Yet I do not deny this article. Acknowledging and affirming the legitimacy and validity of our own interpretations as male European-American exegetes is, as will become clear in chapters 2, 3, and 4, a necessary condition for accountability and, actually, for true repentance. But Paris is right: Outside of a "repentance-framework," despite its good intentions, this proposal would lead us to sin.

4. Elisabeth Schüssler Fiorenza, "The Ethics of Interpretation: De-Centering Biblical Scholarship," *Journal of Biblical Literature* (1988) 107:3–17.

5. Schüssler Fiorenza, "The Ethics of Interpretation" 14–15. It might be useful to clarify the vocabulary here. The "choice of the theoretical interpretive models" is a matter of ethical *responsibility;* discussing the "ethical consequences of the biblical text and its meanings" is a matter of ethical *accountability.*

6. Ibid., 15.

7. Elisabeth Schüssler Fiorenza, *In Memory of Her: A Feminist Theological Reconstruction of Christian Origins* (New York: Crossroad, 1983), xxi. See also Walter Wink, *The Bible in Human Transformation: Toward a New Paradigm for Biblical Study* (Philadelphia: Fortress Press, 1973).

8. I presuppose here the discussion of the following chapters (see esp. chapter 3) in which I argue that male European-American interests and concerns, in and of themselves (i.e., when properly conceived from my perspective as a Protestant male European-American), do not conflict with the interests and concerns of other groups; the problem is with their absolutization—not an easier problem. For instance, the "liberal Protestant" *male European-American* interests and concerns in overcoming the devastating effects of dogmatism and fundamentalism (e.g., exclusion, oppression, sectarianism) demand that we reject patriarchalism and oppression in all its forms. The androcentrism (or patriarchalism) and Eurocentrism of our critical exegetical practices are *in contradiction to our own interests and concerns.*

9. This is what happens in the other "sciences" according to Thomas Kuhn, *The Structure of Scientific Revolutions*, 2d ed. (Chicago and London: University of Chicago Press, 1970). Although many objections have been made to Kuhn's proposal, its main argument is confirmed by the work of René Thom in mathematics (his theory of "catastrophes"): R. Thom, *Modèles Mathématiques de la morphogenèse* (Paris: Bourgeois, 1980) and *Paraboles et catastrophes* (Paris: Flammarion, 1983). See also Jean Petitot, *Les catastrophes de la parole: de R. Jakobson à R. Thom* (Paris: Maloine, 1985). Petitot shows how this "paradigm shift occurred in theories regarding language, communication, and semantics.

10. For a concise presentation of these theories, see Thomas W. Ogletree, *The Use of the Bible in Christian Ethics* (Philadelphia: Fortress Press, 1983), 15–45. Contrary to Ogletree, I do not seek to integrate these theories into a single comprehensive one. I acknowledge their distinctiveness. Consequently, I advocate going through several ethical moves (from chapter 1 to chapter 4, and back again), reflecting one theory or another.

11. Or "teleological." This branch of ethical theories finds expression in utilitarianism: e.g., David Lyons, *The Forms and Limits of Utilitarianism* (New York and London: Oxford University Press, 1965). Through its emphasis on the intentional structure of action and intentionality, it is closely related to phenomenology.

12. Compare Immanuel Kant, *Fundamental Principles of the Metaphysics of Morals* (New York: Bobbs Merrill, 1949).

13. See, for instance, Stanley Hauerwas, *Character and the Christian Life: A Study in Theological Ethics* (San Antonio, Tex.: Trinity University Press, 1975), and idem, *A Community of Character: Toward a Constructive Christian Social Ethics* (Notre Dame and London: University of Notre Dame Press, 1981).

14. My understanding of ethics and ethical theories was also somewhat eclectically shaped by Bruce Birch and Larry Rasmussen, *Bible and Ethics in the Christian Life* (Minneapolis: Augsburg, 1976); Dan O. Via, Jr., *The Ethics of Mark's Gospel in the Middle of Time* (Philadelphia: Fortress Press, 1985); Jeffrey Stout, *Ethics after Babel: The Languages of Morals and Their Discontents* (Boston: Beacon, 1988); Wayne C. Booth, *Critical Understanding: The Powers and Limits of Pluralism* (Chicago: University of Chicago Press, 1979); and idem, *The Company We Keep: An Ethics of Fiction* (Berkeley: University of California Press, 1988); Darrell J. Flashing, *The Ethical Challenge of Auschwitz and Hiroshima: Apocalypse or Utopia?* (Albany: SUNY Press, 1993); Thomas L. Schubeck, *Liberation Ethics: Sources, Models, and Norms* (Minneapolis: Fortress Press, 1993); as well as, in a very different and significant way, by Peter J. Paris, *The Social Teaching of the Black Churches* (Philadelphia: Fortress Press, 1985); Sharon D. Welch, *Communities of Resistance and Solidarity: A Feminist Theology of Liberation* (Maryknoll, N.Y.: Orbis, 1985); idem, *A Feminist Ethic of Risk* (Minneapolis: Fortress Press, 1990); Cornel West, "Ethics and Actions in Frederic Jameson's Marxist Hermeneutics," in *Postmodernism and Politics* (Minneapolis: University of Minnesota Press, 1985), 123–44; and Gayatri C. Spivak, "Scattered Speculations on the Question of Value," *Diacritics*, 1985, 15:73–93.

15. In this, I follow Marcel, Lévinas, and Ricoeur. See Gabriel Marcel, *The Mystery of Being*, 2 vols. (Chicago: Henry Regnery, 1950); and idem, *The Existential Background of Human Dignity* (Cambridge: Harvard University Press, 1963). Emmanuel Lévinas, *Totality and Infinity: An Essay on Exteriority* (Pittsburgh: Duquesne University Press, 1969); idem, *Otherwise than Being or Beyond Essence* (The Hague: Martinus Nijhoff, 1981); idem, *Ethics and Infinity* (Pittsburgh: Duquesne University Press, 1985); idem, "De l'éthique à l'exégèse," *Les Nouveaus Cahiers* 82 (Automne 1985); and idem, *Time and the Other* (Pittsburgh: Duquesne University Press). Paul Ricoeur, *Oneself as Another* (Chicago and London: University of Chicago Press, 1992).

16. This is a point that I argued long ago, following Gabriel Marcel; see Daniel Patte, *L'Athéisme d'un Chrétien ou un Chrétien à l'écoute de Sartre* (Paris: Nouvelles Editions Latines, 1965).

1. Assuming Responsibility for Our Biblical Interpretations

My suggestion in the Introduction, that our present exegetical practices as male European-Americans are ethically problematic, may have been, I suspect, surprising for many of my colleagues. For us there has been no serious ethical problem with our current exegetical practices. Thus, for those still holding this view, this book might seem to be a fanciful quest for a solution to a nonexistent problem.

But this problem does exist. It can be perceived, however, only if our conception of "ethics in critical exegesis" is transformed. In this chapter, I explain first how my paradigm shift regarding this issue occurred and how I progressively discovered that my critical work negatively affects people with other perspectives. I had to assume responsibility for this. As the reality of this ethical problem appeared, questions of its nature and sources arose. Finally, I conclude that affirming the legitimacy of a multiplicity of varying interpretations seems to be the only possible solution to this problem.

Ethical Responsibility and Critical Exegesis: Shifting Perceptions

The issue of ethical responsibility in biblical interpretation has traditionally been strictly limited to the way in which one uses or abuses critical methods in the study of the biblical text. Rigorously studying the text as a historical object by following strict critical methods was implementing the "morality of knowledge" demanded by the Academy and the guild of biblical scholars;[1] interpretations based upon textual evidence adduced through the use of these critical methods are trustworthy (rather than deceitful). This was also assuming our ethical responsibility as biblical scholars to our students and all other people who benefited from our work: our rigorous critical exegeses elucidated the true meaning of the text for our contemporaries and thus made it possible for them to, first, read this text correctly, by rejecting their inadequate uncritical readings, and then to proceed to develop appropriate hermeneutical interpretations. This view was corroborated for us by the positive responses to our work from many quarters, including those who were liberated from the blinders their uncritical readings constituted. In sum, for me, ethical responsibility toward the Academy (morality of knowledge) and toward those affected by our work was identical with rigorous critical study of the biblical text through the application of appropriate methods.

For me, and many other biblical scholars, ethical problems were exclusively methodological problems: ethical irresponsibility was the use of an inappropriate methodology; unethical behavior was the misuse of a methodology (i.e., its artificial use for reading one's own views into the text). These could be serious problems, yet their resolutions merely demanded close attention to methodological issues. Consequently, methodological research was a primary concern—an ethical concern.

This collective methodological research had an unexpected effect. Instead of leading to the establishment of "the" definitive and authoritative methodology (and its morality of knowledge), it led to a methodological explosion. Very diverse critical methods were developed and introduced in biblical studies. For instance, literary, narrative, semiotic, structural, sociological, and anthropological methods found their place in biblical studies beside the historical methods, such as textual, form, redaction, and tradition criticisms. With many others, I was soon convinced that all these methods are "critical" in the strong sense of the term: They follow rigorous criteria defined by a specific methodology. Yet, with the help of Van Harvey,[2] I also noted that they involve quite different "moralities of knowledge" (ultimately based on different ontologies and epistemologies). What counts as trustworthy evidence varies from one method to another. Furthermore, these methods provoke conflicts of interpretations: they reach quite different conclusions regarding each given text.

Until about 1980, it was possible to resolve the methodological confrontations either by rejecting as irresponsible one of the methodologies and affirming the other as the only legitimate one (as many did) or by envisioning their complementary roles in the comprehensive critical interpretation of a given text (as I did at that point).[3] But the number of these constantly recurring confrontations, the progressive critical refinement of the newer methods (preventing their outright rejection), and the growing awareness of the incompatibility of the interpretations resulting from different methods (preventing their integration into the comprehensive critical interpretation) dashed any hope of maintaining as a goal for biblical criticism the establishment of a unified overall methodology. One was (is) confronted with a plurality of coexisting authoritative methodologies and thus with a plurality of moralities of knowledge. Nevertheless, the conception of ethical responsibility remained unchanged; the Academy and the guild continued to act as guardians of morality of knowledge, even though there was now a plurality of specific moralities (and methodologies).

Such an uncertain and self-contradictory equilibrium cannot be maintained indefinitely. The shift of paradigm began to occur in various areas. Deconstructionist[4] and reader-response critics[5] emphasized the relativity of any given interpretation, and the role of the readers in the production of meaning (with the text or out of it)—in accord with key aspects of earlier works by specialists in hermeneutics (especially Martin Heidegger,[6] Hans-Georg Gadamer[7] and Paul Ricoeur[8]). Simultaneously, semioticians (such as Umberto Eco[9] and A. J. Greimas)[10] produced semiotic theories that sought to account for the production of meaning through the entire communication process (including enunciator and enunciatee, and even actual author and actual readers) with, as a result, a strong emphasis on the polysemy of any text. More precisely, these semioticians (especially Greimas) underscored the plurality of quite distinct structured dimensions in any given text—each dimension offering to readers the possibility of perceiving a coherent meaning for the text.

Of course, many resist and will continue to resist the introduction into biblical criticism of these deconstructionist, reader-response, and semiotic theories. But a growing number of exegetes are convinced, as I also am, of the necessity of introducing these approaches in biblical criticism, although without knowing where this might lead.

For me, accepting this shift of paradigm (limited at that point to the methodological level) has freed me to study a single dimension of biblical texts in my studies of Paul's letters and of the Gospel according to Matthew.[11] Yet, despite my explicit warnings that I was studying a single dimension of the texts, which I called their "systems of convictions," my books were often read as if they were studies of *the* entire meaning of the text. I do not want to blame my readers. In doing this, they were seizing on one dimension of my texts that reflected my own uncertainty about the significance of singling out for study a given dimension of a biblical text. Did I not at least imply that the "system of convictions" of a text is its most fundamental and significant dimension?

The second volume of my work on Matthew was to provide a systematic presentation of Matthew's convictions, as well as an explanation of the relationship of this dimension to other dimensions of Matthew's text. Thus, as I began preparing it, I had to envision a multidimensional study so as to prevent the confusion that resulted from my preceding works. But, the paradigm shift had not yet fully occurred for me. I still imagined emphasizing the greater significance of one of these: the system of convictions. I had not yet perceived the implications of these methodological moves for the conception of the ethics of interpretation in biblical criticism.

A first step in that direction came for me as a result of being confronted by Peter Haas with the ethical implications of the horrors of the Holocaust.[12] After much resistance and denial, I had to acknowledge, painful as it was, that my studies of Paul and Matthew, despite their explicit rejection of anti-Jewish interpretations, still conveyed anti-Judaistic (latent anti-Semitic) sentiments.[13]

My ethical responsibility as a critical exegete appeared in a new light; exegesis is not merely a matter of the rigorous use of critical methods. Besides my accountability to the Academy and the guild, I am also accountable to Jews who suffer discrimination by Christians, including discrimination at the hands of my readers whom, without realizing it, I encouraged to be anti-Jewish. Although not intentionally, and often against our intentional efforts to fight and prevent anti-Jewish interpretations of the New Testament, we Christian exegetes too often end up promoting anti-Judaism in a subtle and thus, unfortunately, most effective way. The nature of the subtle anti-Judaism of many of our exegetical studies (related to the form of our arguments rather than to their content) is discussed in chapter 2. Here it is enough to note that we fail to be accountable to our Jewish brothers and sisters. In the process, I noted that anti-Jewish readings were based on a given dimension of the texts, while other dimensions did not provide a basis for such readings. Yet, I could not do much more than begin to realize that ethical responsibility in biblical criticism might require a multidimensional study.

Almost simultaneously, another confrontation forced me to recognize the much broader scope of our ethical responsibility in our failure to be accountable to those who are directly or indirectly affected by our work and teaching. This confrontation came from African-American students at the Divinity School at Vanderbilt University. Over the years, the admission of African-American students had been encouraged, and we rejoiced at their growing number. African-American professors had been appointed. Several courses included study of the African-American church traditions. Yet the content and form of other courses (e.g., biblical studies) were not affected by the presence of African-American students. Like any other students, they needed to be introduced to the critical study of the Bible, didn't they? But, following one particular incident, they openly expressed how our teaching affected them: It demanded from them the denial of their own experience and identity as members of the African-American community and churches; our teaching was thus fundamentally racist.[14]

I took this blunt accusation quite personally; it meant that my teaching in New Testament was fundamentally racist. After initial denials, I realized that they had to be right; I could not deny how African-American students were affected by my teaching. As my practice of critical exegesis (in research and teaching) involuntarily conveyed anti-Judaism, so it involuntarily discriminated against African-Americans, demanding that they abandon their own identity, experience, and concerns.

This acknowledgment led me to the further realization that I had so far avoided being truly confronted by the charge of feminist scholars and students that the practices of male exegetes are fundamentally patriarchal. In response to this charge, I had of course learned to use gender-inclusive language. I had also included in my courses the reading of works by feminist scholars; but these readings were not really integrated into the courses, and thus they challenged the very form of these courses.

Elisabeth Schüssler Fiorenza[15] helped me begin to perceive that all this is a matter of our ethical accountability. Critical exegetes must be accountable to all those who are directly and indirectly affected by their work and teaching, as well as to the Academy and the guild for the critical character of their work. From the perspective of this new understanding of ethical responsibility and accountability in critical exegesis, it is clear that we male European-American exegetes are not accountable to those who are affected by our work. The seriousness of the ethical problem that we have to confront is now fully apparent.

Should we not question the integrity of exegetical practices that ultimately demand that Christian feminists, African-Americans, third-world churches, Jews, and many other groups (potentially, anyone who is not a European-American male) renounce their own experiences and their own cultures, forsake their own identities, and deny the validity of their own concerns and interests? Our ethical accountability as male European-American exegetes can no longer be ignored in the present situation.[16] In this situation, third-world churches rapidly develop to the point of encompassing the majority of the Christians in the world, a development due in large part to their proclamation of the Christian faith in terms of their own cultures (and no longer in terms of the Western culture)[17] and in terms of the crying need for justice. In this situation, the African-American churches and their unique characteristics are increasingly acknowledged and respected wherever the fruits of the Civil Rights movement are allowed to mature into a true reciprocal relationship in which European-American churches and their exegetes slowly (too slowly) are led to recognize that they have much to learn from the African-American churches. In this situation, feminist critics make us aware of the distinctive and central roles and places of women in the development and maintenance of Christian communities that systematically alienated them and continue to alienate them by denying their authority and their identity as women. And finally, in this situation, Jewish scholars, by calling us to join them in remembering the Holocaust, lead us to acknowledge that the anti-Judaism embedded in the New Testament is not a benign and inconsequential feature of these texts, but latent anti-Semitism that easily becomes virulent anti-Semitism.

In such situations as these, how can we ignore our ethical responsibility for exegeses that deny any validity to the experiences, cultural identities, and ethical concerns of these groups? Ignoring this responsibility would make us fail to be accountable not only to all these groups but also to European-American males whom, against the very goal of our teaching, we would condemn to continue to practice injustice and discrimination, to continue to be oppressors, and thus to be alienated from these many brothers and sisters.

Such is the compelling ethical problem in critical exegesis that we can no longer escape: We are not accountable to these groups.

The recognition of this problem raises questions about the ethical responsibility of critical exegetes. What does shifting the conception of ethical responsibility entail? Does the acknowledgment that our exegeses need to be accountable to those who are directly or indirectly affected by our work mean that we should no longer be accountable to the Academy? Schüssler Fiorenza carefully emphasizes the need for both kinds of accountability.[18] But as soon as one seeks to envision how to address the ethical problem identified above, these two kinds of accountability appear to be incompatible.[19]

For me not so long ago, the renunciation of my own experience and culture, the forsaking of my identity, and the denial of the validity of my concerns and interests was not a problem (ethical or otherwise). It is what critical exegesis is all about. Critical exegesis should strive to be disinterested, shouldn't it? Is it not true that one has to bracket out one's concerns and interests so as to elucidate as objectively as possible "what the text meant"? Did we not renounce our own concerns and interests so as to practice critical exegesis? So, what could be wrong about asking the same thing from students?

These questions explain why we, male European-American critical exegetes, did not perceive this ethical problem: Our conception of what it is to be "critical" prevented us from seeing. In other words, the

paradigm shift concerning our conception of ethical responsibility entails a shift concerning our conception of "criticism" and "critical exegesis." The necessity of this shift progressively imposed itself upon me
as, together with many others, I tried to envision how to be accountable to those affected by our work as male European-American critical
exegetes.

The Quest for a Solution

The nature of the ethical problem in (male European-American) exegesis is not easy to elucidate because of the emotional character of the
many issues under consideration. Assuming responsibility for the lack
of accountability of our exegetical practices involves acknowledging
the validity of the cries of those for whom our exegetical practices are
racist, sexist, anti-Jewish, or colonialist.[20] But this acknowledgment
often engenders guilt, which hides rather than reveals the nature of the
problem and leads us to devise inappropriate solutions that compound
rather than resolve the problem. This was my own experience, which
seems to be typical.[21]

My first inclination was to correct the practices for which I felt
guilty by striving to make my exegetical work "pro-woman," "pro-
African-American," and so forth. In my exegetical work and in my
teaching I sought to address their concerns. But it soon appeared that
this was not an appropriate solution: Women, African-Americans,
Jews, and others remain as much alienated by such an artificial exegetical effort as by our traditional work—as African-American students at
Vanderbilt let me know in no uncertain terms.[22]

What was wrong? In brief, I conceived of the ethical problem as a
failure to address the difficulties experienced by women, African-
Americans, and other oppressed groups. (Note that the ethical problem has its roots in "their" difficulties; our sin is a "sin of omission.")
Thus, through my corrected and now "righteous" exegetical practices,
I "spoke for them" (on their behalf; e.g., by emphasizing the biblical
themes that support their causes). I should not have been surprised by
the unenthusiastic and often openly negative responses to my well-
intentioned efforts by women, African-Americans, and third-world
students. It was, after all, a patronizing attitude: It placed them in a
subaltern position; I, a European-American male, defined what "their"
problem was and provided appropriate solutions for it. Such practices
perpetuate the ethical problem: All those outside our group are denied
the status of subjects with their own concerns and identities.

When I acknowledged this, it became clear that the ethical problem in our critical exegesis is much more pervasive; it is a structural

problem that affects all our work. But addressing this problem is not easy, because we often fall into another trap. Once again, my experience seems to be typical.

Because I felt guilty about my previous exegetical practices, I decided that I should totally abandon them to adopt a radically new practice—one that I would attempt to learn from feminist and other advocacy scholars. I felt I should "listen to" them so as to learn both the nature of the ethical problem (still conceived as "their" problem) and the way to address it. Thus, I sought to integrate feminist and African-American insights into my own interpretations; I adopted their inclusive language and even some of their procedures and results.

A willingness to learn from feminist and other advocacy scholars seemed most appropriate to me. Because part of the problem was that the critical exegetical practices of male European-Americans exclude as illegitimate (or uncritical) the biblical interpretations of these other groups, should we not now affirm their validity? In the process, we would affirm the validity of their concerns and interests.[23] One way to do so would be to renounce the critical criteria of our exegetical methods by which we exclude their interpretations. This would involve redefining our vocation as a "hermeneutical" rather than an "exegetical" one. Is this not what feminist and other advocacy biblical scholars do when they present their works as "hermeneutics"? Is not this redefinition warranted by deconstruction, reader-response criticism, and the theories about the hermeneutical circle? Are not all interpretations hermeneutical in character, that is, interpretations of "what the text *means for us*"? Thus, should we not abandon critical exegesis and its aspiration to provide an interpretation solidly grounded in the text that excludes uncritical interpretations? Should we not consider our task as a "critical hermeneutics" that would provide a description of the various hermeneutical interpretations of the various groups?

Yet this solution soon appeared to me as problematic as the first one. To begin with, most male European-American exegetes would strongly resist such a proposal because it demands that we abandon our *raison d'être* and our identity as critical exegetes—a signal that this solution is inappropriate. Furthermore, when I claimed that I wanted to "listen to" feminist and other advocacy scholars, I was once again surprised by the negative response from these groups. I finally recognized with their help that through such an approach I was coopting them[24] by pretending that I could renounce my own identity and status (including my status as oppressor), and thus I was essentially denying that racism and patriarchalism in critical exegesis are "my" problems as a male European-American.

Of course, we must bear the responsibility for our ethical failure; but this does not mean that we have to act out of guilt. We have much to learn from feminist, African-American, and other advocacy scholars, but we will learn it only by "speaking *with* them" in a dialogue in which each respects the otherness of the others.[25] Yet to initiate such a true dialogue is far from easy. Before we can acknowledge and respect the otherness of others, we European-American males must acknowledge and respect our own otherness.[26] Thus, though we have ears, we do not hear (cf. Matt. 13:13–15; Rom. 11:7–8) the distinctiveness of the utterances of others; so against our best intentions, we often revert to "speaking for them" (patronizing them) or "listening to them" (coopting them).

"Speaking with them" is possible only after a shift of paradigm on our part, as was the case regarding our perception of the ethical problem itself. The difficulty of this shift of paradigm and its nature becomes even clearer when we consider next what feminist, African-American, and other advocacy scholars tell us regarding the source of our failure in accountability.

The Androcentrism and Eurocentrism of Our Exegetical Practices

What should we learn about our own practices as we dialogue with feminist, African-American, and other advocacy scholars? What are they telling us about our practices? For me, their most important point is that the fundamental problem with our so-called neutral or objective practices of critical exegesis is that they are androcentric (often patriarchal)[27] and Eurocentric.[28] These terms express the fact that the male and European perspectives, approaches, methods, and interpretations are taken to be normative and universal and therefore posited as the only legitimate ones. We European-American males are thus accused of taking as absolute what is not absolute. We are accused of idolatry.[29] Our sin is a twofold idolatry: androcentrism and Eurocentrism.

My own interpretation of Paul's teaching,[30] clarifies the validity of this accusation. One of the consequences of idolatry, whatever might be its nature, is the corruption of human relations (e.g., Rom. 1:18–32; Gal. 4:8–9; 5:15, 19–21). Accordingly, the idolatrous character of our critical exegetical practices would explain why they corrupt human relations through racism and patriarchalism, and in other ways. Our failure to be accountable to those affected by our idolatries and our destruction, oppression, and alienation of such groups will continue as long as we are in bondage to these two idols. So we see how serious the problem of our lack of accountability in critical exegesis is; freeing oneself from one's idolatry is not an easy task. Actually, Paul emphasizes

that one cannot free oneself alone; an intervention of the Other is
needed.

But are we really trapped in these idolatries? It took me a long time
to acknowledge that I was and that I continue to be trapped in them
again and again. I was quick to admit guilt for specific androcentric and
Eurocentric practices that I struggled to correct by speaking for or listening to those that I had hurt by these practices. It was a matter of refining and purifying specific exegetical practices by making sure that
my rigorous use of critical methods would take into account the concerns of feminists and other advocacy scholars. But the more I struggled to eradicate androcentrism, patriarchalism, Eurocentrism, and
racism from my critical practices in my research and in the classroom,
the more feminist and other advocacy scholars and students accused
me of androcentrism and Eurocentrism. Thus, as I reexamined myself,
I soon found other specific practices that needed to be corrected . . .
and the cycle was beginning again. As Paul said: "I do not understand
my own actions. For I do not do what I want, but I do the very thing I
hate" (Rom. 7:15).

The problem was that I was seeking to correct specific androcentric
and Eurocentric practices from the perspective of an overall practice
that was itself androcentric and Eurocentric. The more we try to overcome androcentric and Eurocentric practices, the more we pretend
that our perspective is neutral (nongendered, nonclassist, nonracial,
and noncultural), and the more we absolutize our male and European
perspective.

From this experience and Paul's description of idolatry, we should at
least learn that being freed from our bondage to androcentrism and
Eurocentrism does not involve rejecting our male and European perspectives.[31] According to Paul, as those Jews and Jewish Christians who
had made of Torah an idol should not reject Torah, so we should not
reject our "maleness" and our "Europeanness." Torah was and contin-
ues to be a good gift from God: it is holy, just, and good (Rom. 7:12),
insofar as it is not absolutized. Similarly, our maleness and Europeanness are good gifts from God, so long as we do not transform them into
destructive idols. It is the idolatry alone that needs to be rejected.
Thus, according to this interpretation of Paul, we must not only acknowledge but also claim our own "maleness" and "Europeanness,"
provided that we do so in a "critical" way that prevents their absolutization. This is what I call an "androcritical" attitude. Then, it is hoped,
we can be ourselves. We will no longer feel the need to coopt the work
of feminist and African-American scholars.

My interpretation of Paul's teaching also convinced me that abandoning my androcentric and Eurocentric idolatries is not something I

can do by myself; it demands the acknowledgment of the role of the Other (and of "others" in their otherness) in my own experience—including in our interpretations. Finally, my interpretation of Paul's teaching makes it clear that overcoming the idolatrous character of my critical exegetical practices is something that I must first do for my own sake, and not only for the sake of those negatively affected by my work. As a result, my patronizing tendencies would be kept in check.

Toward an Ethically Responsible Exegetical Practice: From One-Dimensional to Multidimensional Exegesis

Adopting such an androcritical attitude means that we should reject or abandon *neither* our male European-American perspective *nor* our own critical vocation, which finds expression in our critical exegetical methods. Yet our *practices* of these methods, and thus our conception of what "critical" exegetical practices entail, should be completely reoriented: They must allow us to affirm the legitimacy of a plurality of interpretations—both our own and those of various other groups. If we do so, our interpretations will no longer be androcentric and Eurocentric; we will no longer implicitly or explicitly claim that our own interpretations (whatever they are) are universal—because they strive to establish the single true meaning of the text. But how can we envision such critical exegetical practices?

Here, for me, the work of Mieke Bal was decisive.[32] On the basis of semiotic theories, she examines the history of scholarship on Judges 4 and 5, a series of quite different, yet critical, studies of the same text. Taking advantage of the fact that this text includes two parallel stories of Sisera's death (though her proposal applies to any text), she does not seek to show, as is usually done in a critical review of the scholarship, that the very different interpretations of Sisera's death are partially or totally illegitimate (since they result in incompatible interpretations). Rather, she demonstrates that each of these interpretations is as coherent (it accounts for the text as a whole) and critical (legitimate) as the others. For this, she convincingly argues that the differences among these interpretations come from the choice of different "codes" as foci of the critical investigations (the historical, theological, anthropological, or literary code). Each of these codes reflects concerns and interests of certain groups in specific contexts and is studied through the use of a specific critical method. Having established this point, Bal is in a position to acknowledge that each of the "semantic coherences" of the text emphasized by the different critical exegeses is critically legitimate, provided that the exegeses do not make universal claims. Then she can argue for the legitimacy of using other codes (the thematic and gender codes that represent the concerns and interests of other groups) for interpreting the text.

Bal's work[33] allowed me to understand the significance of Greimas's insistence that any given text is to be conceived of as a plurality of quite distinct structured "meaning-producing dimensions."[34] Each of these meaning-producing dimensions offers readers the possibility of perceiving a coherent meaning for the text. Different readers, because of their specific interests, concerns, or backgrounds, perceive different yet coherent meanings in a text (or better, produce these meanings with the text) by selecting one of these dimensions of the text. Thus, a diversity of readings corresponding to the diversity of meaning-producing dimensions of a text can be viewed as potentially legitimate from a semiotic perspective (and also from a historical perspective, as we shall see below).[35]

One can then envision that the ethical problem in critical exegesis comes from the fact that its "one-dimensional" practices are each conceived as a quest for *the* (single, universally true) semantic coherence of a text. The solution to the ethical problem posed by a one-dimensional critical exegesis appears to be the practice of a "multidimensional critical exegesis."[36]

This proposal does not demand from us that we abandon our traditional view of our vocation (as chapter 3 discusses); it is still a critical exegesis (rather than a hermeneutics) establishing the legitimacy of interpretations by verifying that they are truly based upon textual evidence and account for a semantic coherence of a given text. But for most of us, the proposed "multidimensional critical exegesis" does not appear to be plausible. Is it not a self-contradiction to say that a "critical exegesis" should be "multidimensional"? The claim by semioticians (Bal and Greimas) that a text is multidimensional[37]—the basis for this proposal—does not establish the plausibility of such a conception of a text for those who are not semioticians. Does one need to become a semiotician in order to be ethically responsible as a critical exegete? Of course not. What is at stake is a different understanding of the *practice* of critical exegesis, which can be perceived as plausible from the standpoint of any methodology. The only requirement is that we not absolutize our own methodology and thus that we acknowledge the legitimacy of other methodologies. These are the issues that I address in chapter 2.

Yet for another group of male European-American scholars (reader-response and deconstructionist critics), as well as for feminist and other advocacy scholars, this proposal is not plausible, although for opposite reasons: They find suspicious the insistence that a critical study of the Bible should continue to be conceived as an "exegesis" aimed at establishing legitimate interpretations. Why not define the task of biblical scholarship as a hermeneutical task or as a reader-response criticism? For the reasons mentioned, these suggestions are inappropriate for most male European-American exegetes. The denials of our past exegetical work, and even of our identity, that would be necessary for such a redefinition would lead us to duplicate and perpetuate the ethical problem while pretending to address it. As usual, we would deny the contextual character of our own interpretations—our own perspective as male European-American exegetes. What is needed is a practice of biblical study that accounts for the multiplicity of readings, related to the variety of contexts from which readers read (as the proponents of the various kinds of reader-response criticism emphasize), and also accounts through a "critical exegesis" for the role of the text in the process of reading. A multidimensional critical exegesis, in addition to being based on a plausible view of texts, provides the possibility of accounting for the multiplicity of readings and of recognizing their basic legitimacy.

Are Multidimensional Critical Exegetical Practices Plausible?

This suggestion, and its explanation in chapter 2, will not alleviate all the suspicions that the proponents of biblical scholarship as hermeneutics might have toward a multidimensional conception of critical exegesis. And rightfully so. A multidimensional critical exegesis is not in itself a solution to the ethical problem posed by the critical exegetical practices of male European-American exegetes. I underscore in chapter 3 that this "multidimensional exegetical practice" must also be an "androcritical" (contextual) practice, which begins with a critical examination of our own current practices and interpretations as male European-American exegetes. Yet before explaining this latter point, I would need to show the plausibility of conceiving of critical exegesis as multidimensional. The difficulty is that, once again, this plausibility cannot be demonstrated; it will be perceived when the paradigm shift that has transformed our view of ethical responsibility affects other issues.

First, our view of the nature of the "critical interpretation of a text" needs to be transformed so that we might envision the possibility that several different readings are equally legitimate—a perspective without which one cannot conceive of a multidimensional critical exegesis. The question is, What prevents us from recognizing the plausibility of a multidimensional exegesis? Is it an inability to conceive of a text as polysemic, or better, as made up of a multiplicity of meaning-producing dimensions (a conception which is a necessary presupposition for any multidimensional exegesis)? We can already see that this is certainly not the case, since from the perspective of the traditional paradigm we base our critical exegetical methods on critical methodologies[38] that acknowledge the polysemy of many kinds of texts and therefore the potential legitimacy of a plurality of readings. Neither is it an issue concerning the *kind* of critical methodologies and methods we use in our critical exegeses. Rather, it is an issue concerning the role of methodologies and methods in critical exegetical practices. This observation allows us to recognize that envisioning as "critical" a multidimensional exegesis that affirms the equal legitimacy of different readings will occur only insofar as we undergo *a paradigm shift concerning our perception of the roles of different methodologies and our perception of the relationship among the resulting conflicting readings.* This is the issue I address in chapter 2.

A second issue concerns the conception of critical exegetical practices that would truly be ethically accountable to *both* the Academy *and* those who are directly or indirectly affected by it. I anticipate that male European-American exegetes will think that such multidimensional practices amount to abdicating our "critical" responsibility to the Academy. This concern is not unfounded; certain inappropriate forms of multidimensional interpretive practice would have just this unwanted effect. Conversely, I anticipate that feminist and other advocacy scholars will be rightfully suspicious of multidimensional practices by male European-American exegetes: Will they simply be another means for male European-Americans to oppress other groups? Certainly some inappropriate forms of multidimensional practices are as ethically problematic as one-dimensional practices. Envisioning a multidimensional critical practice that will be ethically accountable to both the Academy and those affected by it demands a paradigm shift concerning our perception of the critical task of exegetes, so much so that it might be possible to conceive of it as both critical and "interested."

Such issues seem to invite a theoretical discussion. Yet it is better to be more concrete, since a paradigm shift occurs only when one is confronted by concrete problems that the old paradigm cannot address. Consequently, in the following chapters, in order to clarify why multidimensional critical exegetical practices are plausible, I once again adopt a narrative style: I describe concrete issues that convinced me of the plausibility of such exegetical practices.

NOTES

1. See the description of the historical methodology as a "morality of knowledge" in Van Harvey, *The Historian and the Believer: A Confrontation between the Modern Historian's Principles of Judgment and the Christian's Will-to-Believe* (New York: Macmillan Co., 1966), 102 ff. Yet the fact that each methodology provides a distinct "morality of knowledge" will raise questions that challenge this perspective.

2. Harvey emphasizes the relationship between methodology and "morality of knowledge." Consequently, different methodologies posit different "moralities of knowledge." See Harvey, 102ff.

3. See D. Patte, *What Is Structural Exegesis?* (Philadelphia: Fortress Press, 1976), 1–20.

4. For implications of deconstructionism for biblical studies, see Gary A. Phillips, ed., *Poststructural Criticism and the Bible: Text/History/Discourse, Semeia 51* (Atlanta: Scholars Press, 1990); David H. Fisher, "Self in Text, Text in Self," *Poststructural Criticism*, 137–54; and Phillips's essays, "Exegesis as Critical Praxis: Reclaiming History and Text from a Postmodern Perspective," *Poststructural Criticism*, 7–49; and "Sign/Text/Différance: The Contribution of Intertextual Theory to Biblical Criticism," *Intertextuality* (Berlin: de Gruyter, 1991), 78–101. See also David Jobling and Stephen D. Moore, eds. *Poststructuralism as Exegesis, Semeia 54* (Atlanta: Scholars Press, 1992), esp. Fred Burnett, "The Undecidability of the Proper Name 'Jesus' in Matthew" (123–144).

5. For examples of reader-response criticism, see Robert Detweiler, ed. *Reader-Response Approaches to Biblical and Secular Texts, Semeia 31* (Atlanta: Scholars Press, 1985), including the articles by Robert M. Fowler, "Who Is 'the Reader' in Reader Response Criticism?" (5–23); Janice Capel Anderson, "Double and Triple Stories, the Implied Reader, and Redundancy in Matthew" (71–89); Fred W. Burnett, "Prolegomenon to Reading Matthew's Eschatological Discourse: Redundancy and the Education of the Reader in Matthew" (91–109); Gary Phillips, "History and Text: The Reader in Context in Matthew's Parables Discourse" (111–38). See also Robert M. Fowler, *Let the Reader Understand: Reader-Response Criticism and the Gospel of Mark* (Minneapolis: Fortress Press, 1991).

6. M. Heidegger, *Being and Time* (London: SCM, 1962).

7. H. G. Gadamer, *Truth and Method* (New York: Seabury Press, 1975).

8. Among his many works addressing this issue, see esp.: Paul Ricoeur, *The Conflict of Interpretations: Essays in Hermeneutics* (Evanston, Ill.: Northwestern University Press, 1974).

9. See esp. Umberto Eco, *A Theory of Semiotics* (Bloomington: Indiana University Press, 1978); and idem, *The Role of the Reader* (Bloomington: Indiana University Press, 1979).

10. See esp. the comprehensive work in which he brings together the several discrete works on specific aspects of the semiotic phenomenon: A. J. Greimas and J. Courtès, *Semiotics and Language: An Analytical Dictionary* (Bloomington: Indiana University Press, 1982; original French, 1979). For a systematic introduction to Greimas's semiotics, see D. Patte, *Religious Dimensions of Biblical Texts: Greimas's Structural Semiotics and Biblical Exegesis* (Atlanta: Scholars Press, 1990).

11. See D. Patte, *Paul's Faith and the Power of the Gospel: A Structural Introduction to Paul's Letters* (Minneapolis: Fortress Press, 1983), 1–30, 190–231, passim, where I emphasize the distinction between Paul's system of convictions (the dimension that I study) and his theology (another dimension); and idem, *The Gospel according to Matthew: A Structural Commentary on Matthew's Faith* (Philadelphia: Fortress Press, 1987), 1–13, passim, where I make similar distinctions and underscore (in italics) that I deal with a single dimension of the text.

12. See Peter Haas, *Morality after Auschwitz: The Radical Challenge of the Nazi Ethic* (Philadelphia: Fortress Press, 1988). It is not by chance that Haas's work had such an effect on me. The Holocaust is part of the context from which I write, having been in contact with Jewish refugees (whom my parents helped to escape) during World War II in France and being married to a woman who, unlike other members of her family, escaped it.

13. D. Patte, "Anti-Semitism in the New Testament: Confronting the Dark Side of Paul's and Matthew's Teaching," in "The New Testament and Judaica/ Judaism," *Chicago Theological Seminary Register,* 78.1 (1988) 31–52.

14. A charge which, for me, was later confirmed and clarified by the following books (see esp. their introductions): Cain Hope Felder, *Troubling Biblical Water: Race, Class, and Family* (Maryknoll, N.Y.: Orbis Books, 1989); and Cain Hope Felder, ed. *Stony the Road We Trod: African American Biblical Interpretation* (Minneapolis: Fortress Press, 1991).

15. E. Schüssler Fiorenza, "The Ethics of Interpretation."

16. A situation in which, as Larry Rasmussen writes, "Christianity has shifted decisively from the religion of the rich to the faith of the poor, and the vitality of Christian faith has passed from the European and North American world to peoples in Africa, Latin America, and Asia, to the women's movement most everywhere, and to communities in our own midst who are in touch with these" (*Christianity and Crisis,* May 16, 1988).

17. For instance in Africa, the large majority of Christians belong to "independent churches" (such as the Kibanguist churches in the Congo and Zaire, and the Zionist churches in Southern Africa).

18. E. Schüssler Fiorenza, "The Ethics of Interpretation."

19. This question is not raised in Christopher Rowland and Mark Corner, *Liberating Exegesis: The Challenge of Liberation Theology to Biblical Studies.* (Louisville, Ky.: Westminster/John Knox, 1989). This work bypasses the question of the status of critical exegesis and many of the other questions that arise out of my deliberate attempt to raise them from my perspective as a male European-American exegete. Rowland and Corner's distinctive contribution is to elucidate the questions that are raised by the uses of the Bible in liberation theology, which they carefully analyze.

20. I became aware of the colonialist character of our exegeses when students from Africa (where I lived for two years) led me to read post-colonialist studies as well as works on African religious traditions. See Edward W. Said, *Orientalism* (New York: Pantheon, 1978); idem, *The World, the Text, and the Critic* (Cambridge: Harvard University Press, 1983); and idem, *Culture and Imperialism* (New York: Alfred Knopf 1994); Kwame Anthony Appiah, *In My Father's House: Africa in the Philosophy of Culture* (New York and Oxford: Oxford University Press, 1992); Laura E.

Donaldson, *Decolonizing Feminisms: Race, Gender, and Empire-Building* (Chapel Hill and London: University of North Carolina Press, 1992); Itumeleng J. Mosala, *Biblical Hermeneutics and Black Theology in South Africa* (Grand Rapids: Wm. B. Eerdmans Publishing Co., 1989); André Karamaga, *L'Evangile en Afrique: Ruptures et continuité* (Yens/Morges: Cabédita, 1990). See also the broader work by R. S. Sugirtharajah, ed., *Voices from the Margin: Interpreting the Bible in the Third World* (Maryknoll, N.Y.: Orbis Books, 1991).

21. My experience corresponds to the analytical categories, "speaking for others," "listening to them," and "speaking to them" (or, better, "speaking with them") proposed by Gayatii C. Spivak to describe typical attitudes of people toward those they consider as subalterns. Spivak proposed these categories in her study of the "representations" (either political "speaking for" [*vertretung*] or artistic or philosophical re-presentation [*darstellung*] following a "listening to") of women as subaltern subjects in colonial India by British authorities or artists and philosophers (as undeconstructed subjects). "Speaking with" does not exclude representation but takes place when the process of subject-construction (both that of the speaker and that of the one who is spoken to) and the "interests" involved are made explicit. From my perspective, "speaking with the other" happens when one simultaneously recognizes the otherness of the other and affirms it by recognizing, thanks to it, one's own otherness, i.e., one's own different identity. See Gayatri C. Spivak, "Can the Subaltern Speak?" in *Marxism and the Interpretation of Culture*, ed. G. Nelson and L. Grossberg (London: Macmillan Co., 1988), 277–313 (esp. 295). See also Spivak, *In Other Worlds* (New York: Methuen, 1987), esp. "French Feminism in an International Frame," 134–53. Spivak's categories are used by Western biblical scholars in South Africa, especially Jill Arnett, "Feminism, Post-Structuralism and the Third World: An Assessment of Some Aspects of the Work of Gayatri Spivak," (unpublished paper, Critical Studies Group, University of Natal at Pietermaritzburg); and Gerald West, *Contextual Bible Study* (Pietermaritzburg: Cluster Publications, 1993), esp. 14–17, yet the rest of the book is an implementation of "speaking with (ordinary readers)." See also Gerald O. West, *Biblical Hermeneutics of Liberation: Modes of Reading the Bible in the South African Context* (Pietermaritzburg, South Africa: Cluster Publications, 1991). Furthermore, this was also the experience of the male European-American scholars who participated in the conference on "ethical responsibilities and practices in biblical criticism" sponsored by the Lilly Endowment and held at Vanderbilt University in March 1991. Once again, let me underscore that the insights in this section have been thought through with Gary Phillips and are as much his as mine.

22. It should be clear that these comments do not deny that male European-American exegetes have the responsibility for elucidating in the Bible the themes and issues of justice for the oppressed. This is what Norman Gottwald has done in an exemplary way in all his work, including *The Tribes of Yahweh: A Sociology of the Religion of Liberated Israel, 1250–1050 B.C.E.* (Maryknoll, N.Y.: Orbis Books, 1979); and what is acknowledged by the publication of David Jobling, Peggy L. Day, Gerald T. Sheppard, eds., *The Bible and the Politics of Exegesis: Essays in Honor of Norman K. Gottwald on His Sixty-fifth Birthday* (Cleveland: Pilgrim Press, 1991). The problem has to do with the way in which we perform these studies (our practice). It is

one thing for us to study the themes and issues of justice, because it is "their" problem as poor and oppressed, but it is quite another thing to study it as "our" problem. This better practice is exemplified by multivoiced publications, such as
Norman Gottwald and Richard Horsley, eds., *The Bible and Liberation: Political and
Social Hermeneutics* (Maryknoll, N.Y.: Orbis Books, 1993); and Willy Schottroff
and Wolfgang Stegemann, eds., *God of the Lowly: Socio-Historical Interpretations of
the Bible* (Maryknoll, N.Y.: Orbis Books, 1984). The condition is, of course, that
they do not fall into the next trap: being content to "listen to" others.

23. This is the overall approach of Rowland and Corner (*Liberating Exegesis*),
which, at one point, I thought was the appropriate response. What follows explains
why I abandoned it. As David Rensberger expresses it in a review, their work is "beyond exegesis and hermeneutics." For me (unlike Rensberger), this is a part of the
problem. Yet, once again, the work of Rowland and Corner remains very helpful.

24. As feminist, womanist, mujerista, African-American, and Hispanic-American
scholars emphasized at the above-mentioned Vanderbilt conference in March
1991.

25. Cf. the discussion of the different types of relation to the "other" in Enrique
Dussel, *Philosophy of Liberation* (Maryknoll, N.Y.: Orbis Books) ch. 2, "From Phenomenology to Liberation," 16–66, where the author challenges the "centered-
ness" and the structure of "sameness" of North Atlantic ontology. See also the
works by Marcel, Levinas, and Ricoeur cited in n. 14 of the introduction, above.

26. See Ricoeur, *Oneself as Another*, 113–68, passim.

27. As feminists have long stressed. See Schüssler Fiorenza, *In Memory of Her*.

28. Cf. Felder, *Stony the Road We Trod*, 6–7.

29. An accusation which is explicitly made, for instance, in *The Road to Damascus: Kairos and Conversion*, a document signed by Third-World Christians from El
Salvador, Guatemala, Korea, Namibia, Nicaragua, Philippines, South Africa (London: CIIR, Washington: Center of Concern, London: Christian Aid, 1989).

30. See, Patte *Paul's Faith*, 257–77 (on Rom. 1:18–22 and 7:7–25).

31. This is what Gary Phillips and I expressed in "A Fundamental Condition for
Ethical Accountability in the Teaching of the Bible by White Male Exegetes: Re-
covering and Claiming the Specificity of Our Perspective," *Scriptura: Journal of
Bible and Theology in Southern Africa*, Special Issue S9 (1992), 7–28.

32. Esp. Mieke Bal, *Murder and Difference: Gender, Genre, and Scholarship on Sisera's Death* (Bloomington: Indiana University Press, 1988). See also Mieke Bal,
Lethal Love: Feminist Literary Readings of Biblical Love Stories (Bloomington: Indiana
University Press, 1987); and idem, *Death and Dissymmetry: The Politics of Coherence
in the Book of Judges* (Chicago and London: University of Chicago Press, 1988).

33. Bal's above-mentioned works, and also Mieke Bal, *Narratology: Introduction
to the Theory of Narrative* (Toronto and Buffalo: University of Toronto Press, 1985).

34. A phrase that I use to express what Greimas underscores in his semiotic theory (a metatheory that is best designated as a semio-literary theory, since it provides
an overall model accounting for a great diversity of literary theories) by speaking of
"meaning" as a "meaning-effect" produced ("generated") by readers with a multidimensional text, or by speaking of the phenomenon of "textualization" (how a
"meaningful text" is produced by readers on the basis of one or another of the

dimensions). See Greimas and Courtès, *Semiotics and Language*, 133–34, 187–88, 287–93, 341, passim; and Patte, *Religious Dimensions of Biblical Texts* (the entire book is focused on this issue). Although, following Greimas, I emphasize therein four broad meaning-producing dimensions, it should be clear that these are actually categories of dimensions, each including quite a number of more specific structured dimensions, as the concluding and more technical part of the book explains.

35. Bal's point in *Murder and Difference*, regarding the diverse scholarly interpretations of Judges 4 and 5, can be illustrated by considering the diversity of recent interpretations of any biblical text. For instance, about the different scholarly interpretations of the Gospel according to Luke, one could say, of course, that one of these different interpretations is right and that all the others are wrong. This is what is usually done in review articles or in the introductory chapter of a new scholarly work. Yet one can recognize, following Bal, that through the use of different methodologies, the different studies elucidate different "codes"—or what I prefer to call different "meaning-producing dimensions." But we can go even one step further. Below, I pair studies using the same methodologies that reach quite different conclusions regarding the significance of the text. Does this mean that one is right and the other wrong? Actually, it could be shown that they focus on different features of the text, on different subcodes, that I would still consider to be different "meaning-producing dimensions."

Thus, Jean-Noël Aletti (*L'art de raconter Jésus Christ: L'écriture narrative de l'évangile de Luc* [Paris: Seuil, 1989]), Robert C. Tannehill (*The Narrative Unity of Luke-Acts: A Literary Interpretation, Volume 1: The Gospel according to Luke* [Philadelphia: Fortress Press, 1986]), and John Darr (*On Character Building: The Reader and the Rhetoric of Characterization in Luke-Acts* [Louisville, Ky.: Westminster/John Knox, 1992]) use a narrative/rhetorical methodology; but because they define it in different ways, they elucidate different dimensions of the Gospel and reach different conclusions regarding its significance. Similarly, Jean Delorme (*Au risque de la parole: Lire les évangiles* [Paris: Seuil, 1991]), 93–124; and Daniel Patte (*Structural Exegesis for New Testament Critics* [Minneapolis: Fortress Press, 1990] 99–118), propose two "semantic" analyses, which are different, because they are focused on distinct semantic features (figurativization and thematization, respectively). Agnès Gueuret, *L'engendrement d'un récit: L'évangile de l'enfance selon saint Luc* (Paris: Cerf, 1983), and Louis Panier, *La naissance du fils de Dieu: Sémiotique et théologie discursive. Lecture de Luc 1–2* (Paris: Cerf, 1991) analyze the discursivization of the text, but from two different perspectives, and thus focus on distinct codes. Finally, Jane Schaberg, "Luke," in *The Women's Bible Commentary*, Carol Newsom and Sharon Ringe, eds. (Louisville: Westminster/John Knox; London: SPCK, 1992) 275–92; idem, *The Illegitimacy of Jesus* (New York: Crossroad, 1990); and Raymond E. Brown, *The Birth of the Messiah: A Commentary on the Infancy Narratives in Matthew and Luke* (Garden City, N.Y.: Doubleday, 1977), both of whom use literary-historical approaches, obviously consider different meaning-producing dimensions! Otherwise, they could not support with evidence contradictory conclusions.

36. For short examples of "multidimensional exegeses" that affirm the legitimacy of several different (and even contradictory) readings, see Timothy B.

Cargal, "'His Blood Be Upon Us and Upon Our Children': A Matthean Double Entendre?" *NTS* 37 (1991) 101–12; and Daniel Patte, "Bringing Out of the Gospel-Treasure What Is New and What Is Old: Two Parables in Matthew 18–23," *Quarterly Review* 10/3 (1990) 79–108.

37. This is also the claim of postmodern critics, such as Michel de Certeau, *Heterologies: Discourse on the Other* (Minneapolis: University of Minnesota Press, 1986); and Jay Clayton, *The Pleasures of Babel: Contemporary American Literature and Theory* (New York and Oxford: Oxford University Press, 1993).

38. I presuppose a clear distinction between "methodology" and "method." As I use it in this book, a methodology is the theoretical basis (including an epistemology) of a set of critical methods. I limit my discussion to two methodologies: the historiographical methodology (that encompasses the traditional historical-critical methods) and the semio-literary methodology (that encompasses most recent literary and semio-structural methods). Despite their great diversity, they share the same kind of epistemology. Other methodologies (such as the sociological-anthropological one) are no less important. They are not discussed here simply because their status is not clear for me. Although at times they are presented as independent methodologies, they are often conceived as subcategories of the historiographical (in the case of sociological methodologies) or semio-structural methodologies (in the case of anthropological ones).

2. A Quest for Accountability: Multidimensional Exegetical Practices

Chapter 1 has shown the ethical urgency of envisioning a different kind of critical exegetical practice. This appears to us, male European-American exegetes, when we become aware through a paradigm shift that ethical responsibility includes accountability not merely to the Academy, but also to those affected by our work. Since our primary failure concerns our accountability to those who have interpretations different from ours, I proposed that the way of correcting this ethical failure might be exegetical practices that would affirm the legitimacy of different interpretations—multidimensional practices. Yet the plausibility of this proposal is far from obvious: It will make sense only insofar as we undergo a paradigm shift concerning our perception of the roles of different methodologies and our perception of the relationship among the resulting conflicting readings.

This paradigm shift happened to me as I strove to determine how to study and teach "discipleship" according to the Gospel of Matthew while preparing a book on this topic[1] and searching for a way of teaching that would be accountable to the very diverse students in my classes. Thus, once again, I tell the story of how my perception of the practice of critical exegesis was progressively transformed, so much so that I could accept the plausbility of "multidimensional" and "interested" critical exegetical practices. This is also how I envisioned the *possibility* that multidimensional critical practices would be ethically accountable provided that their "interested" character be clearly acknowledged.

"Go and Teach" but "You Shall Not Be Called Masters": The Multidimensionality of a Text

My study of discipleship began with the deliberate identification and investigation of tensions among components of the teaching about

37

discipleship in the Gospel according to Matthew and in the scholarship
on it. In so doing, I was still following a traditional exegetical practice:
According to the old paradigm, the perception of a tension between
two teachings about discipleship signals either a lack of textual unity
(e.g., due to the redactor's use of different sources or traditions) or a
lack of understanding on the part of exegetes of the (single) coherence
of the text, and is thus a problem to be resolved. The study of a text
progresses when, instead of hastily accepting the traditional resolutions
of these tensions, one takes the time to "size them up" and allows oneself to be puzzled by them. Still, according to the old paradigm, in
many instances one should accept that the text includes such tensions.
Respecting the textual evidence demands that we renounce resolving
these tensions and thus recognize that a text includes a plurality of dimensions, each with its distinctive semantic coherence. For instance,
according to a historiographical methodology, these tensions might
signal the use of two different sources. In sum, whatever the methodology in use might be, traditional critical exegetical practices already
acknowledge that a plurality of textual dimensions provides the basis
for a plurality of different legitimate readings of a given text.

The shift from the traditional paradigm to the new one concerns the
way in which one assesses the relative authority of these different legitimate readings. According to traditional practices, the relative authority of these various readings is *decidable* on critical grounds. By
contrast, as I struggled with these texts and with the ethical question, I
progressively discovered that the relative authority of these various
readings is *undecidable* on critical grounds, and thus must be decided on
other grounds—that is, according to the concerns and interests of the
exegete and his or her group, as I discuss below.

This point is best explained by considering a first tension in the
Gospel according to Matthew. This tension is particularly relevant because it directly concerns the ethical problem posed by our current
critical practices and because it exemplifies the need for acknowledging that a text is multidimensional.

The Tension

Disciples are people whose vocation includes preaching (the gospel
of the kingdom, Matt. 10:7) and teaching ("to observe all that I have
commanded you," 28:20) with authority (received from Jesus who
sends them, 28:19). How is this to be reconciled with passages such as
Matt. 23:8–11: "But you are not to be called rabbi, for you have one
teacher, and you are all students. And call no one your father on earth,
for you have one Father—the one in heaven. Nor are you to be called

instructors, for you have one instructor, the Messiah. The greatest among you will be your servant"?[2]

A Traditional Interpretation

A first type of interpretation proposes to resolve this tension by, for instance, reasoning such as this: Matthew 23:8–11 does not deny the use of authority per se. It demands that disciples be "servants" and thus that they use authority "for others,"[3] rather than for their own benefit (e.g., for honorific treatments). But it remains that disciples as preachers and teachers (10:7; 28:20) have a special status (they are commissioned by Jesus), a special access to the truth (that they, unlike others, have directly received from Jesus), and thus they have a special authority to which others must submit. In sum, other followers of Jesus must submit to the disciples as preachers and teachers.

A Feminist Response

For many Christian feminists, this interpretation (and the churches and exegetes who adopt it) is a source of "great scandal" (cf. Matt. 18:6–7),[4] because it betrays the teaching of 23:8–11 and justifies all kinds of patriarchal behavior.[5] In the process of resolving the tension, the traditional interpretation, above, favors passages such as 10:7 and 28:20, and dismisses the challenge posed by 23:8–11 by reading it in terms of these other passages. Feminists, however, demand that we take 23:8–11 on its own terms, and then the tension appears in all its sharpness. In 23:8–11, we find what Schüssler Fiorenza calls a "discipleship of equals"; by contrast in 10:7 and 28:20, the focus of the preceding interpretation, we find an "authoritarian-patriarchal discipleship" (disciples as "masters"). This tension cannot be resolved. One needs to acknowledge that it is generated by the presence in the text of two dimensions with different, coherent views of discipleship.

Such an identification of different dimensions in a text is not new in biblical scholarship. Historical-critical methods such as form criticism and redaction criticism have long acknowledged the presence of such tensions in the Gospel according to Matthew. According to these methods, the tensions reflect the use of traditions or sources by the redactor, and thus the presence of several textual dimensions, or historical strata. Thus, Schüssler Fiorenza, and other historical-critical exegetes, ascribes the conception of a "discipleship of equals" to early traditions that go back to the historical Jesus, and ascribes the patriarchal and hierarchical view of discipleship to the redactor, Matthew.[6] The tension in the text is respected. Then two kinds of readings, each emphasizing one view of discipleship, are equally legitimate. The pre-Matthean traditions and the Matthean redaction are equally well grounded on textual evidence. *The text of the Gospel carries two contradictory messages about discipleship in its two historical dimensions.*

Such a historical-critical practice acknowledges, therefore, a plurality of textual dimensions and of legitimate critical readings. This is what one finds in the commentaries using this methodology when they discuss, for instance, the "meaning" of the beatitudes according to Jesus, according to early church traditions, according to the source Q, according to the Sermon on the Mount (for Hans Dieter Betz), as well as according to Matthew as redactor (see, e.g., the studies of the Sermon on the Mount by Georg Strecker,[7] Ulrich Luz,[8] W. D. Davies and Dale Allison,[9] and Betz,[10] each of which involves a distinction between at least two historical strata). Other critical methods (those derived from semio-literary methodologies) also recognize a plurality of textual dimensions, each with its distinct semantic coherence (see chapter 1).

This critical acknowledgment of a plurality of textual dimensions and of legitimate readings is not the "multidimensional exegetical practice" that is called for in order to correct the problem of our lack of accountability. As we examine more closely Schüssler Fiorenza's feminist interpretation of the tension between "Go and teach" and "You shall not be called master," it becomes clear that, in order to be accountable to the various people affected by our work, our multidimensional practice must make explicit that all the textual dimensions and all the legitimate readings have *equal authority.* Yet this nonhierarchical conception of textual dimensions and of readings makes sense only as we shift paradigm by reflecting upon the conditions for teaching according to the model of a discipleship of equals.

Ethical Accountability in Teaching and Critical Methodologies: Discipleship of Equals and Male European-American Exegetes

Schüssler Fiorenza claims that a "discipleship of equals" is the conception of discipleship that "empowers us [women] to walk upright, freed from the double oppression of societal and religious sexism and prejudice." Yet it is a conception of discipleship that "still needs to be discovered and realized by women and men today."[11] According to her, in order to be accountable to those affected by our work, male European-American exegetes should envision their exegetical practices according to the "discipleship of equals model."[12] I fully agree. But, to my surprise, I progressively discovered that practicing exegesis according to the discipleship of equals model demands that we make explicit that the alternate reading of Matthew (authoritarian-patriarchal discipleship) is equally authoritative. This appeared to me as I asked myself these questions: How should a discipleship of equals be envisioned in the case of disciples who are called to teach (Matt. 28:18–19)? How should our pedagogical practices according to this model be conceived? And thus, how should we conceive of the role of methodologies in our exegetical and pedagogical practices?

When disciples preach and teach, they do exercise authority. But how can they do so without usurping the authority of the heavenly Father or of Christ, that is, without implicitly or explicitly presenting themselves as "rabbis," "fathers," or "masters" to whom others must submit, by claiming a distinctive status and a special access to the truth? The issue is this: What kind of authority should disciples exercise as they teach in a community of equals?

These questions directly apply to us as interpreters of the Gospel according to Matthew, and especially to us, male European-American exegetes: How can I present a critical exegesis of Matthew in a publication or in a classroom without presenting myself as a teacher who has a unique and universal claim to the truth of this Gospel and thus as a "master" to whose teaching others must submit? This question raises, in a specific case, the central issues concerning our critical exegetical practices.

Take the concrete example of a classroom situation: a diverse student body including women and men from different ethnic, social, economic, cultural and religious backgrounds taught by a male European-American biblical scholar. How could I eventually teach this course without being perceived as a "master"?

A Common Type of Pedagogical Practice in Critical Biblical Studies

Let us first review how I taught a class on the Gospel of Matthew according to the traditional model. I made a point of basing my teaching on the history of scholarship, as well as on the latest publications on Matthew. I referred to these works in my lectures and in the discussions as I presented Matthew's view (singular) of discipleship. I referred to dissimilar critical interpretations and to the scholarly debates, but I soon took a side in these debates, arguing for the greater critical plausibility of one kind of interpretation over the others. Even if I argued in favor of the interpretation of a leading scholar rather than for my own (as a way of expressing that I am not one of the "masters"), I was necessarily perceived by the students as presenting the authoritative interpretation of Matthew, and thus as presenting myself as a "master" (who has a "critical" mastery of the text).

Consequently, even when I used an interactive pedagogy, the students were reduced to the role of passive receivers of my teaching. They were implicitly posited as unable to propose a legitimate interpretation on their own, so long as they were not "formed" by me and thus so long as they did not conform their ways of interpreting the Gospel to mine by becoming the "same" as me.[13] Was it not appropriate to transform students into "critical readers" of the Bible like myself? Consequently, they were required to deny any value to their (uncritical) interpretations and to their ways of interpreting that reflected their concerns, their interests, and their (positive or negative) experiences, as, for example, members of one or another church or group in different cultural and social contexts. Consequently, European-American women, African-American, Hispanic-American and third-world women and men, and even European-American men from backgrounds different from the teacher's, were required to deny value to their own identities.

This type of pedagogical exegetical practice is a clear instance of the problem in ethical accountability that I described in chapter 1. By (consciously or not) presenting himself as master, the teacher condones, perpetuates and subtly advocates oppression and discrimination. His teaching as a critical scholar to whom students must submit duplicates the structure of oppression that manifests itself in patriarchalism and sexism, but also in racism, anti-Semitism, and cultural and economic oppressions.

Of course, this analytical description of a common kind of exegetical pedagogical practice is quite sketchy. But I hope it is not perceived as a caricature. I simply underscore the quandary in which I found myself when I examined my twofold responsibility of being accountable to the Academy (by being "critical") and accountable to those who are affected by my work. If we strive to be critical exegetes, how can we avoid being perceived as masters by uncritical readers whom we try to educate? How else could we teach critical biblical studies to students who arrive in class with uncritical (and often quite vague) readings of the Bible?

The answer to this question depends on our conception of what constitutes a "critical" interpretation of a "text." As long as we conceive of the text as one-dimensional (that is, as having a single true meaning or as emphasizing a single meaning as the most authoritative), our critical exegetical task can only be conceived of as a quest for *the* single, true, authoritative meaning of the text—as a one-dimensional exegesis. Then we have predetermined that our teaching will offer *the* true interpretation or *the* way to the true interpretation, to which others must submit and conform. Consequently, the structure of our teaching cannot help but be a structure of oppression.

An Alternative Type of Pedagogical Practice

Our ethical accountability to those who are affected by our exegetical work demands that we take seriously the injunction, "You shall not be called masters." We cannot afford to ignore it. Yet the question remains: How can we present in our writings or in the classroom a critical exegesis of Matthew without claiming for ourselves a unique "mastery" of the text? My (partial) answer:[14] through a multidimensional practice of critical exegesis that would present as equally legitimate and equally authoritative different readings of the text.

Ironically, this would mean that, in order to take seriously in our exegetical practices the injunction, "You shall not be called masters," we should present as equally legitimate and authoritative both readings of it: (1) the reading that underscores *the discipleship of equals* by its focus on Matt. 23:8–11 (and similar instructions) and by its interpretation of the disciples-teachers' authority (expressed in Matt. 10:7 and 28:20) as a nonhierarchical, egalitarian relationship; and (2) the reading that underscores the *hierarchical view of authority* by its focus on Matt. 10:7 and 28:20 (and similar instructions) and by its interpretation of Matt. 23:8–11 in this perspective. Such a multidimensional practice would be accountable to those affected by our exegetical work, as becomes clear when we envision the type of pedagogical practices that would implement it.

If the male European-American teacher of a diverse group of students would offer such a multidimensional teaching, his pedagogical practice would no longer be a metaphor for oppression. He would not claim "mastery of the text."[15] On the contrary, he would present himself as confronted by two different and incompatible teachings of a text that he cannot master.

Consequently, those to whom he would address this multidimensional teaching would not be reduced to the role of passive receivers of his interpretation. They would be posited as active and responsible participants in the interpretative process. Since the two Matthean teachings, which would be presented as equally legitimate and authoritative, are incompatible, in order to "make sense of the text" for themselves, the students would have to make a choice. On what ground? Obviously, this choice would not be dictated either by the multidimensional critical exegesis or by the text. Thus, they would have to make this choice in terms of the concerns and interests arising out of their own specific experiences and identities, which they would no longer be required to abandon or deny. Prior to the multidimensional critical teaching, they might or might not have made the same choice. If they were now to make a different choice, they would do so, not because it would be required by the teacher as master, but because of their own concerns. They might discover, in the critical light provided by the class, that their prior interpretation was actually at odds with their own concerns. Even if they were to make the same choice as before, such multidimensional critical teaching would have a significant effect for them: They would choose to hold to their original reading with the critical awareness of what they are doing and of the grounds upon which they are doing it.

I present this alternative pedagogical practice in critical biblical studies in a conditional form, because the way to implement it still needs to be envisioned.[16] Such a practice would, indeed, satisfy the requirements for accountability toward those affected by our work. But would it satisfy the requirements for accountability toward the Academy, the requirements of critical studies? It does. In order to see that it does, one needs to note that such a multidimensional practice has two requirements: (1) recognizing that a given text includes several different semantic dimensions and (2) presenting several interpretations as equally legitimate and authoritative, so much so that the choice among these interpretations would not be predetermined by the critical exegeses themselves.

The first requirement is plausible from the perspective of critical exegesis. Far from forsaking the respect of the text that characterizes the critical stance, the recognition of several dimensions in a text accurately represents the text. It acknowledges the presence of tensions in the text (e.g., between two views of discipleship) and respects them by taking them as signals that the text includes several semantic dimensions. Such an exegetical and pedagogical practice respects the text as it makes explicit these tensions (rather than resolving them) and presents both of their sides as equally legitimate readings of the text. Such a practice is, therefore, truly critical, as is made explicit through the use of different critical methods for the study of each of the dimensions. For example, these dimensions might be historical strata, including several "tradition-strata" studied through source, form, and tradition criticisms, and the redaction-stratum studied through redaction criticism. We can even say that one-dimensional interpretations that resolve the tensions ultimately fail to be truly critical; they misrepresent the text by presenting its teaching about discipleship as "unified" when it is not.[17]

The second requirement is far less plausible for critical exegetes. This becomes clear as soon as we consider our actual practices, which remain "one-dimensional" even as we acknowledge the multidimensionality of the text.

Equally Legitimate and Authoritative
Textual Dimensions and Readings

The presentation of several textual dimensions is often found in traditional critical studies, which nevertheless remain one-dimensional exegetical practices. Even though these studies recognize several textual dimensions (and thus, several legitimate readings established through the use of several critical methods), they revert to a one-dimensional exegesis by assigning different degrees of authority to the different dimensions. Consequently, one has no choice but to select the reading based on the dimension with the greater authority.

Historical-critical exegeses, for instance, are most often practiced in this way.[18] They do identify two (or more) historical dimensions of the text (different historical strata), each carrying a distinct teaching about discipleship: in our example, a discipleship of equals and an authoritarian patriarchal discipleship, respectively. Yet the way in which critical exegetical methods, in this case, historical-critical methods, are used prevents any possibility that these two teachings might be viewed as having equal weight. For instance, Schüssler Fiorenza shows, in *In Memory of Her*,[19] that the one can be traced back to Jesus and that the other originates with the redactor Matthew. Is there any doubt regarding which of the two teachings will be viewed as true and authoritative by Christian readers of her exegetical work? Of course, Jesus' teaching carries more weight than Matthew's. The critical exegesis has chosen for its readers. This is still a one-dimensional exegesis. The hierarchical structure remains.

What is needed is an exegesis that would not make this choice for those to whom our exegetical work is addressed, but would rather represent the two (or more) possibilities offered by the text as having equal legitimacy and authority. This would be a truly multidimensional exegesis.

Such a multidimensional exegesis can be envisioned when one notes that, in one-dimensional exegeses, any given methodology establishes a hierarchy among the dimensions that are identified through the use of several critical methods that belong to this methodology. For instance, the historical-critical methodology used by Schüssler Fiorenza establishes a certain hierarchy between the discipleship of equals and the authoritarian-patriarchal discipleship, by identifying (through the use of form, redaction, and sociological criticisms) the former with an early tradition that can eventually be traced back to the historical Jesus and the latter with Matthew's view.

How does this hierarchization of the dimensions, which is a value judgment, occur? A critical study is supposed to be value neutral. But is it really? The hierarchization of the dimensions seems to be intrinsic to the historical-critical methodology used by Schüssler Fiorenza. By ascribing the discipleship of equals to Jesus' teaching and the authoritarian-patriarchal discipleship to Matthew's view, the historical-critical study has predetermined the value judgment of these dimensions. Jesus' words are more important than Matthew's, because Jesus is more important than Matthew for Christian believers, and also because, according to a common view of history, what is more ancient is more important and thus more authoritative. Historiography itself does not demand this value judgment; it can also be practiced by historians who conceive of history in terms of progress (with a reversal of the value judgment); the use of historical-critical methods for the identification of the two dimensions is itself value free. Yet, practicing historical-critical studies in a given cultural context characterized by a specific view of history necessarily establishes a hierarchy among the textual dimensions identified; such a critical exegetical practice is "value loaded."

Since the same could be said about the use of critical methods based upon a semio-literary (or any other) critical methodology, this observation can be formulated as a general principle:

> In a certain cultural context, the use of a given critical methodology, besides providing exegetes with the critical methods necessary for identifying several textual dimensions, predetermines the value judgment of these dimensions, posits their hierarchization, and thus engenders a one-dimensional exegesis.

Yet this hierarchization changes when one uses different methodologies, as one feels free to do when one recognizes that any methodology is culturally conditioned. It follows that

> The use of several methodologies in a single exegetical practice would lead to the conclusion that several dimensions and several distinct readings of a text are equally legitimate and authoritative and thus engenders a multidimensional exegesis.[20]

This preliminary conclusion needs to be explained and justified. The acknowledgment that the hierarchization of dimensions posited through the use of any given critical methodology is culturally bound is, I suspect, less than plausible for many. Those who have been part of the theoretical discussions about methodologies might want to grant in principle that critical methodologies are culturally bound; they are based upon epistemologies that are directly related to the cultural context in which they are developed. But in practice, I believe many of us question the corollary suggestion that a given methodology predetermines the hierarchization of textual dimensions. Is not the hierarchization independent of the critical inquiry, even when it is conducted following a single methodology?[21] For many male European-Americans, this same question is even more direct: How could this hierarchization be predetermined by the methodology in use? Is it not prescribed by the text? Is it not "natural"?

Regarding Schüssler Fiorenza's interpretation of Matt. 23:8–11, I have suggested that the hierarchical relationship between the two dimensions and of the two views of discipleship is posited by the historical-critical methodology and is culturally bound. But is it really possible to conceive of their relationship in any other way? Of course, this is impossible, as long as one exclusively considers this relationship from the perspective of the historical-critical methodology. Yet when this relationship is considered from the perspective of another methodology (for instance, a semio-literary methodology), it is perceived in a quite different way. Actually, the hierarchical relation of the two dimensions is reversed.

To understand this statement, it is enough to take note that historical-critical and semio-literary methodologies include quite distinct conceptions of the phenomenon of "redaction."[22] In both cases, the term "redaction" expresses the interrelation of two components: the process of redaction is the *addition of* "something" (*A*) *to* "something else" (*B*). From the perspective of the historical-critical methodology (and conventional redaction criticism), this relationship is seen as the *addition of* "the redactor's point of view" (*A*) *to* "traditions and/or sources" (*B*). Yet from the perspective of a semio-literary methodology, this relationship is conceived as the *addition of* "something" (*A*) *to* "the redactor's point of view" (*B*).

Historical redaction-critical studies seek to identify how the redactor Matthew has modified sources and traditions by "adding" to them his own view of the disciples and of discipleship (an "addition" that often takes the form of suppressing certain aspects of the sources and traditions).[23] In sum, Matthew's view is "what is added" (*A*); traditions and sources are "what is redacted" (*B*).

By contrast, from a semio-literary perspective[24] the redactional process is conceived as a "discoursivization," that is, as a part of a communication process. Matthew holds certain views (e.g., about discipleship) that he wants to communicate to certain readers (a given church) who do not share his views (e.g., they have a somewhat different view of discipleship) and for whom Matthew's views will be at least somewhat new. In order to be understood and believed by these intended readers, Matthew needs to present his views in terms of what they already know and believe; he needs to "redact" (more precisely, to "discoursivize") his own views. Thus, a successful communication process requires that Matthew "add" something (features from traditions and sources that his readers already know and believe) to his own view about discipleship. In sum, traditions and sources are "what is added" (A); Matthew's view is "what is redacted" (B).

The two meaning-producing dimensions elucidated through the respective critical methods of the two methodologies are similar.[25] In both cases, "what is redacted" and "what is added" are elucidated in comparable ways. In our example, the message about a discipleship of equals is "what is redacted" (or "discoursivized") and the message about an authoritarian-patriarchal discipleship is "what is added." But the hierarchical relationship between the two is quite different because from a historical-critical perspective the discipleship of equals (what is redacted) is attributed to the tradition and ultimately to Jesus, while from a semio-literary perspective it is attributed to Matthew. Similarly, the authoritarian-patriarchal discipleship is attributed to Matthew by the historical-critical methodology and to the tradition (what the implied readers know about Jesus' teaching) by a semio-literary methodology. Consequently, in a cultural situation in which what is from Jesus is more valuable than what is from Matthew (or more generally, in which what is more ancient is more valuable), the hierarchical relationship between the two dimensions and their respective views of discipleship is reversed.

More generally, by using different methodologies one ends up conceiving of the hierarchical relationship among textual dimensions in different ways (as well as perceiving different kinds of textual dimensions). Then, if one would use not one but several methodologies in one's exegetical and pedagogical practices, one would have to concede that the hierarchy among textual dimensions cannot be decided.[26] In our example, when both historical and semio-literary methodologies are used as methodologies with equal status, one cannot decide which is to be attributed to the Jesus-tradition or to Matthew as redactor–author: a discipleship of equals or an authoritarian-patriarchal discipleship. The two dimensions (and their respective views of discipleship) have the same critical status. The relative value of the two is undecidable. As far as critical exegesis is concerned, both are equally legitimate and have an equal claim to be authoritative. Their relationship is value neutral.

Consequently, the pedagogical practices that would present these two dimensions of the Gospel according to Matthew in this way would meet the conditions for accountability to those affected by our work. The male European-American teacher of our earlier example would not present himself as a "master," but rather as someone who has *no* mastery of the text. Students would be free to choose one or the other of these two readings as the meaning of the text for them. In the process each student would, of course, opt for one methodology or another—the one that gives a greater authority to the dimension she or he wants to select.

In sum, when we use several methodologies and respect their differences, acknowledging the critical legitimacy of their different readings, our exegetical and pedagogical practices should become multidimensional and thus accountable to those affected by our work.[27]

The "Interested" Character of Any Given Critical Exegesis: "Love Your Enemies" but "Woe to You, Scribes and Pharisees"

The conclusion that, in order to be accountable to those affected by our work, we need to use several methodologies in our exegetical and pedagogical practices does not mean that we should seek to develop eclectic procedures that would combine the use of several methodologies. On the contrary, it presupposes that each methodology is used with rigor and integrity by applying the specific set of critical methods based on it, so as to develop its distinct series of critical studies of the text. For instance, a historical-critical methodology is, and should continue to be, implemented in a series of studies following, for instance, source, form, redaction, and tradition-critical methods. Similarly, a semio-literary methodology should be implemented in a series of studies following, for instance, literary, narrative, semio-structural, reader-response, and rhetorical-critical methods.

It is only if each methodology, and indeed each of its critical methods, is used on its own that the study is truly critical, that is, consistent in its uses of criteria (although it is always possible to devise a new critical methodological approach by combining critical procedures originating in different methodologies). Different methodologies have different criteria because of their different epistemologies. Thus, for me, it is to be expected and normal that any given critical exegesis uses a single methodology and one (or a few) critical method(s) that belong(s) to this methodology. The multidimensional critical exegesis that I advocate calls for the performance or presentation of a plurality of such critical exegeses, rather than a single one.

Traditionally we exegetes opt for one of the available methodologies and, more specifically, for one or a few of its methods. This is in part because of concrete constraints: It takes much time to develop rigorous critical exegeses of various texts following a given method.

But I want to argue that there is another reason: Opting for a specific methodology and for a critical method is not value free. As Rudolph Bultmann emphasized, the use of a critical methodology amounts to adopting a set of presuppositions, which ultimately are pre-understandings of the text based upon a "life-relation" to the subject matter of the text and reflect an existential encounter with the text.[28] The difference is that, according to Bultmann, exegetes had no choice in methodology (the historical-critical methodology was a sine qua non for critical study of the New Testament), while we now have a choice among several methodologies. In this new situation we can rephrase Bultmann's points by taking note that our choice of methodology (and thus our performance of specific critical exegeses) is "interested." Consequently, it is a fair description of what we are presently doing to say that our specific critical interpretations following a certain critical method are themselves "interested."

Schüssler Fiorenza's work provides an excellent illustration of this point. Her book, *In Memory of Her*, and more precisely her comments on Matt. 23:8–11, is a critical exegetical study using a given methodology, the historical-critical methodology, and more specifically a certain historical-critical method (which combines form, redaction, and sociological criticisms). I have argued that her hierarchization of the semantic dimensions of Matthew is due to the fact that she uses a single methodology. But obviously, her critical work is also an "interested" or "advocacy" interpretation: It is a "feminist critical hermeneutics." Because she has at heart the interests and concerns of women oppressed by sexism and prejudice in both the social and religious realms, she deliberately passes a value judgment upon the two dimensions of the text under discussion from her feminist perspective. Does she betray her critical method in so doing? The preceding discussion shows that, of course, this is not the case (as the rigor of her study further confirms). From my perspective as a male European-American, I conclude that her critical exegetical study in this book uses a certain critical method that belongs to the historical-critical methodology, rather than to another one because it promotes her Christian feminist agenda by ascribing greater authority to the textual dimension that expresses a discipleship of equals.[29]

I do not criticize Schüssler Fiorenza for advocating this view of discipleship. My point concerns the relationship between critical methodologies and interested, or advocacy, interpretations. Far from making an exegesis neutral or disinterested, the use of a specific critical methodology and methods contributes to making the exegesis an advocacy interpretation.[30]

I believe these observations can be generalized: Any given critical exegesis that uses a specific method (belonging to a certain methodol-

ogy) is also an interested interpretation, that is, an interpretation performed in order to address the concerns and interests of a certain
group in a specific social and cultural context.[31]

If it is true that any given critical exegesis using a single (set of) critical method(s) is also an interested interpretation, we would understand one of the causes for one-dimensional critical practices (even
when one recognizes several textual dimensions) and for their lack of
accountability to those affected by these practices. The universalizing
of exegetical interpretations in one-dimensional exegeses would result
from the absolutization of a critical methodology. Thus, one of the
manifestations of the idolatries of Eurocentrism and/or of androcentrism would be our failure to acknowledge the contextual character of
our critical methodologies themselves and, consequently, the interested character of our critical exegeses.[32]

Once again, the suggestion that we should acknowledge the interested character of our critical exegeses is certainly far from plausible
for many male European-American exegetes, although it is self-evident
for feminists and other advocacy biblical scholars. How could I even
imagine that "each given critical exegesis (using a specific [set of] *critical* method[s]) is also an *interested* interpretation"? Is this not self-
contradictory? Have I forgotten what "critical" means? Is there no
longer any distinction between "critical exegeses" and "interested interpretations"? between the study of "what the text meant" (critical exegesis) and the study of "what the text means for us" (hermeneutics)?[33]

Yes, the traditional distinction between critical exegesis and
hermeneutics is blurred.[34] But this does not mean that the critical character of our work as exegetes is to be abandoned. The dichotomy between subject and object is dismissed. But this does not mean that no
distinction is to be made between subject and object; instead of being
either subjective *or* objective (the dichotomy), *either* uncritical *or* critical, each of our critical interpretations can be viewed as both subjective
and objective.[35] A multidimensional practice does not entail forsaking
our vocation as "critical" exegetes: It actually opens the way to carry
out more effectively our vocation as male European-American *critical
exegetes*—as I discuss in chapter 3.

Yet the above objections reflect the perception that, for most of us,
a multidimensional critical exegetical practice once again reflects a paradigm shift: a shift in the conception of the nature and function of
"critical exegesis" and thus of the relationship between our use of critical methods and our vocation as male European-American practitioners of critical exegesis. This shift in perception occurred for me as I
examined two other tensions among aspects of the teaching about discipleship in the Gospel according to Matthew.

"Love Your Enemies," but
"Woe to You, Scribes and Pharisees"

How does one reconcile (*a*) the injunction, "Love your enemies" (Matt. 5:44), with (*b*) the call to reject the scribes and Pharisees (also found in the Sermon on the Mount; cf. Matt. 5:20; 6:2, 5, 16), expressed most virulently in the curse "Woe to you, scribes and Pharisees, hypocrites!" relentlessly repeated in 23:13–29? How does one reconcile (*a*) the presentation of discipleship as servanthood (e.g., 20:25–28), according to which children (18:1–4; 19:13–15) and women (who served and followed Jesus to the cross, unlike the eleven; 27:55–56) are models of discipleship, with (*b*) the patriarchal view of discipleship that pervades the Gospel according to Matthew?

I could not deny the legitimacy of the many exegetical interpretations that perceive the coherence of Matthew's teaching about discipleship in a radical message about love for one's enemies and/or about servanthood, and as a result minimize or ignore the anti-Judaism[36] and/or the patriarchal features of this Gospel.[37] But, simultaneously, I could not deny the legitimacy of exegetical interpretations by other scholars who underscore that anti-Judaism[38] and patriarchalism[39] are integral parts of Matthew's teaching about discipleship. These latter studies cannot be dismissed as "mere advocacy hermeneutics"—by contrast with "truly critical exegeses." The textual evidence underscored by these studies in support of their interpretations is quite strong, as is clear as soon as attention is drawn to it.

As above, these tensions can be explained by the presence of several coherent semantic dimensions in the Gospel according to Matthew.[40] For the moment, I simply want to argue that the very recognition of the existence of these tensions and conflicting interpretations should lead us to acknowledge the possibility that any specific critical exegesis might be an interested, or advocacy, interpretation.

Each of these conflicting interpretations claims to be rigorously critical by referring to strong textual evidence. Yet it is noteworthy that the proponents of the interpretations according to which Matthew's text is anti-Jewish and patriarchal do not hesitate to underscore as an additional argument, beyond the evidence of the text, that this Gospel has been and still is used to justify patriarchalism and anti-Judaism (and even anti-Semitism).[41] They argue that this text has *the effect of conveying patriarchalism and anti-Judaism to its readers*. This is, for these scholars, additional evidence supporting their interpretations. Furthermore, at times they argue that this effect is perpetuated by the interpretations that do not notice how thoroughly intertwined patriarchalism and anti-Judaism are with the so-called radical message of love.

The proponents of the interpretations that emphasize the message of love are then caught in a dilemma. Their critical exegeses show that interpretations underscoring the radical message of love are based upon strong textual evidence. Yet for them, anti-Judaism (as latent anti-Semitism) and patriarchalism (at least in its most obvious manifestations as discrimination and exploitation based on sexism) contradict this message of love. The question is, Why would they not emulate the aforementioned Jewish and feminist scholars and propose as further evidence for the legitimacy of their interpretations that this text has the effect of conveying a radical message of love to its readers? Is it not true that this Gospel has the effect, through its message of radical love, of transforming domineering readers into dedicated participants in the struggle against all kinds of discrimination and oppression? Can we not say about men what Schüssler Fiorenza says about women, namely, that the Bible (including Matthew) "inspires countless women to speak out and to struggle against injustice, exploitation, and stereotyping"?[42] Although the evidence is unfortunately more striking and quite certainly more abundant that Matthew conveys patriarchalism and anti-Judaism, one cannot deny that this text also conveys a message of radical love. As the philosopher Philip Hallie emphasizes in his study of Christians struggling against anti-Semitism and rescuing Jews during World War II,[43] people affected by Matthew's radical message of love existed, even though they were a small minority as compared with the anti-Semites and their many passive accomplices.

These observations suggest that critical exegeses and interested interpretations are closely intertwined. Jewish and feminist critical exegetes are concerned about the negative effects of the Gospel according to Matthew on their respective groups. If it is in their interests to denounce these effects by making them explicit, why would this not be true in the other case as well? I believe that the proponents of the interpretations emphasizing radical love (in most instances, male Christian European-American exegetes) also have something at stake in their interpretations. Are they not also "concerned" about the effects of this Gospel on their own groups?

In the present case, this concern is a positive one (an interest), because the Gospel's effects that they focus on are positive: the transformations of self-centered people into agents of reconciliation. But they might also be concerned (a negative concern) about the fact that the Gospel according to Matthew fails to have this kind of effect on many modern people. Is it not "in the interest of" their groups (Christian European-American communities in which males are in a position of leadership) that such effects of the Gospel be promoted through their interpretations? Is it not also in our interests as male European-

American exegetes, for whom the Gospel according to Matthew is authoritative (as well as a base of our authority) and the source of our livelihood, that this Gospel (and the rest of the Bible) not be viewed as irremediably patriarchal and oppressive? Thus in many different ways, our critical interpretations that focus on Matthew's radical message of love are themselves "advocacy" and "interested" interpretations.

The puzzling question is this: Why have we, male European-American critical exegetes, refused to acknowledge that our specific critical interpretations are interested? We can no longer escape this question. We have managed to do so only so long as we could imagine that the world of legitimate interpretations was limited to our own. Because we can no longer deny the legitimacy of feminist and other advocacy interpretations,[44] we are thus challenged to acknowledge that our own critical interpretations are themselves "interested"—whether or not we were aware of it when we performed them. Furthermore, as soon as we consider this possibility, we are surprised to discover that our own methodological reflections are not against this conception of critical interpretation.

A Pragmatic Conception of Exegesis: The Interested Character of Critical Methods

As I have repeatedly emphasized, the acknowledgment that our critical exegeses themselves have an advocacy character does not demand from us that we abandon or even compromise our commitment to *critical* studies of the Bible. Yet it does demand a paradigm shift regarding the "practical conception" of critical exegesis that we implement in our exegetical practices (rather than a shift in "theoretical conception"). One of the issues that requires a change in our perspective is our conception of what we are doing as we practice critical exegesis.

The basic question is this: Why are we performing critical exegeses? Or better, Why is critical exegeses needed at all?

An answer is presupposed by the negative, polemical character of our traditional, one-dimensional practices of critical exegesis. In brief, we male European American exegetes traditionally perform our critical exegeses in order to reject wrong, uncritical interpretations, such as those of people who bring to the text and read into it their prejudices, which are most often directly related to their interests and concerns.[45] In so doing, we presuppose that by contrast with these interpretations, our critical interpretations are at least partially free from preunderstandings and partially objective; that is, they are presentations of truths about the text (if not presentations of the true meaning of the text) that should be acknowledged by everyone. Otherwise, how could our critical interpretations supplant uncritical interpretations? In this way, our exegetical practices posit that our critical interpretations are disinterested in that they seek to overcome the interested uncritical in-terpretations.

This pragmatic conception implied in our critical practices is in ten-sion with our theoretical awareness that no interpretation, including a critical one, is free from preunderstandings. Who would want to be la-beled a "positivist," after Albert Schweitzer's denunciation of the claims of nineteenth-century historical-critical scholarship?[46] Yet we hold on to the plausibility and legitimacy of this conception of critical exegetical practices by emphasizing that, while absolute objectivity is impossible in historical-critical studies—as Troeltsch already empha-sized in his formulation of the principle of criticism[47]—and a fortiori in literary critical studies, partial objectivity is nevertheless possible; without making an absolute claim, a critical study can nevertheless es-tablish what has a greater degree of probability and thus also what must be rejected because it has a lesser degree of probability.

I do not deny that, through such reasonings, it is possible to estab-lish the plausibility of such a one-dimensional conception of the prac-tice of critical exegesis and its goal. But, once again, I want to claim that another conception of the practice of critical exegesis is at least as plausible as that one. Following the seminal work of Hans-Georg Gadamer (*Truth and Method*),[48] it became clear to a growing number of exegetes that the view of critical exegesis as that through which misun-derstandings caused by preunderstandings ("prejudices," in Gadamer's vocabulary) are avoided was *not* a plausible description of what actually happens in the process of critical interpretation. This traditional view of the role of critical exegesis is particularly challenged by Gadamer's following points:

> Preunderstandings ("prejudices," prejudgments) are conditions nec-essary for understanding, rather than obstacles to proper under-standing or rather than a cause of misunderstandings.[49]

> Interpreting is allowing the claim of the text to provoke a question-ing, which leads the interpreter to enter the "game" of the text and its logic of questions and responses, so much so, as David Tracy says, that "the meaning of the text lies *in front of* the text—in the now *com-mon* question, the now common subject matter of both text and in-terpreter."[50]

> "Understanding is never subjective behaviour toward a given 'ob-ject,' but towards its effective history," and thus a classic text such as the Bible is always interpreted in terms of the history of its effects.[51]

Such analyses of the phenomenon of interpretation show that it is plausible to envision critical exegeses as "interested," simply because any interpretation is interested. Without interests, concerns, life-relations, preunderstandings, prejudgments, presuppositions, and indeed "prejudices," reading, as the interplay between text and reader through which meaning is produced, would not occur. If one were not looking forward with anticipation to something in the text, one would not even open it or would be so bored that the reading would be in vain. Having a preunderstanding of a text, that is, coming to the text with a vested interest, and thus a question or an expectation, does not in itself engender a misreading. In sum, preunderstandings motivate our readings, including our critical readings.

The link between preunderstandings–interests and critical method appears when one notes that, beyond their motivating role, preunderstandings have a direct and positive role in the reading process. It is true that they prevent us from perceiving certain (many) aspects, or dimensions, of the text. Yet they function as binoculars: By narrowing one's vision of the text-landscape, they focus the vision, with the result that one perceives more clearly certain aspects of the text.[52] Preunderstandings–interests focus our attention on a certain dimension of the text so that we see in this dimension what provides the semantic coherence of the text.

We male European-American exegetes should not be surprised by this positive view of preunderstandings–interests, because we pragmatically use it in our works, although usually without acknowledging it. This appears when, instead of speaking of preunderstandings, we speak of the interpreters' hermeneutical concerns and interests.

We are, of course, ready to acknowledge that we perform the critical study of a text because of specific concerns and interests, which we usually qualify as "hermeneutical" so as to preserve the disinterested character of our "critical" exegesis. We do not feel any need to apologize for this. We affirm these hermeneutical concerns and interests. In the introductory parts of our studies, we often express what motivated our research; we study the text in order to address certain questions we have about it—questions which, we presume, also are of concern for others (a certain group that we envision as our readers or audience).

Why, then, could we not acknowledge that we began our *critical study* with the preunderstanding that the text deals with certain issues that need to be clarified? Our formulations of these issues point to our concerns and interests (without necessarily revealing them fully). Furthermore, our description of the critical procedures through which we propose to address these questions discloses that the critical methods themselves are closely related to our concerns and interests. We choose a given critical method rather than another, because in our view it is the most appropriate for addressing the issue we want to deal with.[53] Yet our discussions of the chosen method reveal something else; we are not simply applying this method; in such a case, it would be enough to refer to the appropriate methodological textbook. Rather, we adapt it and *implement it in a specific way* so that it will allow us to deal more directly with the issue that concerns us. In sum, critical methods in themselves are intimately associated with preunderstandings.

Then it is plausible to say that critical methods are formal expressions of certain broad interests and concerns, which are shared by all those who find these methods appropriate: a broad group which, in the case of certain widely accepted critical methods (e.g., text criticism), might include all European-American people and exclude, in our example, people belonging to "oral cultures." In the case of less widely accepted critical methods, it might be simply a segment of the European-American people (e.g., European-American liberals, excluding European-American fundamentalists).[54]

A specific implementation of a given method also embodies preunderstandings: the interests and concerns that are shared by all those who find appropriate this specific implementation of the given method. This is a narrower group, such as the group formed by women in a feminist implementation of this method, or in other implementations, the groups formed by African-Americans, or by liberal European-American males, or even by subgroups of these like Christian European-American feminists or Christian liberal European-American males.[55]

I must, therefore, conclude it is plausible that, far from being free from preunderstandings and far from shielding us from them, critical methods and their specific implementations embody distinctive preunderstandings, concerns, and interests. Critical methods and their implementations do allow us to overcome personal and idiosyncratic preconceptions, as well as the preunderstandings of other groups. They make our interpretations legitimate for a certain group. Yet at the same time, the more rigorously we use a critical method, the more thoroughly our interpretations are governed by the broad concerns and interests represented by this method. Similarly, the more rigorously we practice a given implementation of this method, the more our interpretations are governed by the narrower concerns and interests represented by it.

These conclusions should not surprise us. Note that critical methods in themselves are called "critical" only when they are rigorously defined procedures, that is, when their results (interpretations) can be verified with the help of specific criteria. The definitions and criteria of these methods are themselves established on the basis of a coherent methodology, that is, of a theory (e.g., a historiographical, a semio-literary, or a social-scientific theory). Since any given critical method is based on a theory, and not on an absolute truth, the method is culturally conditioned; consequently, this method represents the view of a certain phenomenon from the perspective, interests, and concerns of a given cultural group at a specific point in history.[56] The fact that a theory provides the basis for concrete and verifiable implementations shows that it is legitimate, but not that it is the only possible theory (which would transcend cultural conditioning). Other theories are also accepted as legitimate when they provide the basis for other concrete and verifiable implementations (through the use of different criteria);[57] they simply emanate from groups in other cultural settings (in different periods or locations).

This legitimacy of a plurality of methodologies (theories) is presently acknowledged by the Academy and the guild.[58] In their collective wisdom, these scholarly bodies pragmatically affirm the legitimacy of several sets of critical methods based on quite different methodologies.[59] Concurrently, scholarly studies of these methodologies show that they include quite different epistemologies reflecting distinct views of the way in which human beings know what they know, and that these theories are related to specific cultural, social, or historical contexts. For instance, the historiographical theory is linked to the industrial revolution and a certain understanding of science;[60] the semio-literary theory is linked to the emergence of the "technological culture."[61] These additional considerations confirm my earlier statement that these sets of critical methods and the theories on which they are based embody and thus serve the interests and concerns of certain groups in specific cultural contexts.

A similar point could be made regarding the specific implementations of each given critical method and the foregoing statement that they embody and serve the interests and concerns of narrower groups. Pragmatically speaking, the Academy and the guild have for an even longer time acknowledged the legitimacy of a diversity of implementations of each critical method. For instance, the method of redaction criticism is practiced in quite different ways in the commentaries by Strecker[62] and Luz[63]—both "good scholarly works" in the estimation of the guild. In both cases, the method itself is quite recognizable: The aim is the elucidation of the redactor's theological views by showing how Matthew redacted the sources (Mark and Q) and the traditions (identified by form-critical studies) he has received. Yet their conclusions are so different that their respective interpretations of Matthew's view of discipleship are incompatible. Why? Is it because one or the other failed to be rigorous enough in his application of the method to the text? Of course not: Both are impeccable exegetes and leading scholars. Both Strecker's and Luz's interpretations are legitimate. The point is that a critical method is never simply "applied." It is implemented in different ways according to the interests, concerns, and thus preunderstandings of the exegete and of a specific group to which he or she belongs.[64]

For us, male European-American exegetes, these considerations should at least show that viewing critical exegeses as interested or advocacy interpretations is at least as plausible as the customary view that says critical exegeses must be disinterested. This shift in our conception of critical exegesis would allow us to envision multidimensional critical practices that would be accountable to the Academy through the rigorous use of a specific methodology and its set of critical methods for each of the several proposed interpretations. Furthermore, if we would acknowledge that the different critical exegeses embody and serve the interests and concerns of specific groups, we would be in a position to affirm the legitimacy of our own interpretations as male European-American exegetes, as well as the legitimacy of those interpretations that are very different from ours, be they proposed by feminist or other advocacy biblical scholars who have at heart the interests and concerns of their distinct groups or by other male European-American exegetes who have at heart interests and concerns of other constituencies. Thus, our multidimensional critical practices (including our pedagogical practices) would be accountable to at least some of those who are affected by our work. But we commonly resist developing exegetical and pedagogical practices that would require an acknowledgment that our critical exegeses are interested.

Multidimensionality as Necessary but Not Sufficient for Accountability in Exegetical Practices

I have attempted to show in this chapter the plausibility of viewing: (*a*) a text as multidimensional, each of the several dimensions offering a semantic coherence that has the potential of becoming the "meaning" of the text for certain readers; (*b*) methodologies (and methods) as giving priority to one or another of these textual dimensions by ascribing a relative authority to each; and (*c*) critical exegeses as interested interpretations. My claim simply is that these three points represent a conception of our usual critical exegetical practices that is as plausible as our traditional conceptions.

Adopting this view is a *necessary* condition for envisioning and developing multidimensional critical exegetical practices (including pedagogical practices) that would be ethically accountable both to the Academy and to those affected by our critical work. But adopting this new perspective is *not sufficient*, as is shown by the fact that we, male European-American exegetes, resist adopting a multidimensional exegetical practice, and that feminist and other advocacy scholars view this proposed solution as suspect. This resistance and suspicion, which were the initial reactions to my proposal, are justified. A multidimensional practice can take many forms that, far from bringing about accountability to both the Academy (usually our primary concern) and those affected by our work (usually the primary concern of advocacy scholars), would betray this twofold goal.

The legitimate suspicion of advocacy scholars and the no less legitimate resistance of male European-American exegetes bring to light two kinds of multidimensional exegetical practices that would be inappropriate because they would fail to be ethically accountable either to those affected by our works or to the Academy. Conversely, an examination of these inappropriate conceptions provide important clues regarding the characteristics that an appropriate multidimensional practice must have.

"Disinterested" Multidimensional Exegetical Practices: A First Inappropriate Conception

Feminist and other advocacy scholars are right to be suspicious of multidimensional practices by male European-American exegetes, as long as it is not clear how and by whom the several textual dimensions studied are selected and what interests govern these multidimensional practices. Multidimensional exegetical practices could easily be misconceived as the establishment *by male European-American critical exegetes* of the several textual dimensions upon which legitimate interpretations of a biblical text can be based.

According to this inadequate model, critical exegetes (unlike other readers) would alone determine the actual meaning-producing dimensions of a text because they would have mastered the various critical methods and methodologies. Following the above suggestions, in such a multidimensional exegetical practice, one would use more than one methodology, thereby elucidating a number of potential meaning-producing dimensions of the text and establishing that no priority could be ascribed to any single one on the basis of a critical study of the text. Thus, one would be in a position to affirm both the legitimacy of all the interpretations based upon any one of these dimensions and the interested character of each of these interpretations.

Conversely, one would be in a position to reject as illegitimate (uncritical) any and all interpretations that were not based upon one of the elucidated dimensions.

For advocacy scholars (as well as for post-modern male European-American scholars), this kind of multidimensional practice would be nothing but another form of androcentric and Eurocentric practice, which owes its multidimensional character to the methodological pluralism of present-day critical exegesis. Indeed, such a practice would be much more "inclusive." It might include the methodological approaches of feminist and other minority scholars, and it might even be totally decentered, that is, no longer centered upon male European-American interpretations seemingly according to Schüssler Fiorenza's wish.[65] Yet this very inclusiveness could mask an effort to coopt minority scholars: Male European-American critical exegetes might try to lure women and other minority scholars to join them in this multidimensional exegetical project by incorporating feminist and other advocacy scholarly works into this broader scholarly framework.

While this might *seem* to us an appropriate way of being accountable to those affected by our works, feminist and other advocacy scholars are quick to point out that such a multidimensional practice would replicate the very lack of accountability it purports to address.[66] The goal of such a practice would still be to establish universally true and normative interpretations of the text, even though this norm would now be a range of several legitimate interpretations. This multidimensional norm would still be used to pass a negative judgment on "uncritical" interpretations, with the effect of demanding from many of those affected by our multidimensional work that they abandon their interpretations and ultimately deny their interests and concerns, and thus their social, cultural, or religious identities.

Part of the problem lies in the fact that, according to this model, multidimensional exegetes would in fact assume the customary position of disinterested critical scholars. While they would emphasize the interested character of each one-dimensional interpretation (including the one they adopt in their private lives), as critical scholars they would set themselves above these interests and concerns by seeking to elucidate and to establish (for everybody) the range of legitimate interpretations of the text under study. Yet the preceding discussion regarding the interested character of one-dimensional critical exegeses also applies to multidimensional critical exegeses. From the point of view of advocacy scholars, despite the implicit claim of disinterestedness embodied in such a practice, there is little doubt that it would in fact be interested. This is a classical case of androcentric and/or Eurocentric biblical criticism, characterized by the denial of its interested character.

From this we can draw a first conclusion.

> Conclusion 1: Appropriate multidimensional critical exegetical practices must make explicit that they are performed in order to address the concerns and interests of a certain group. In our case, they must make explicit their androcritical character, that is, that they seek to address certain male European-American concerns and interests.

Another part of the problem appears to be that such a hypothetical multidimensional practice would maintain a hierarchical pattern between critical exegetes and uncritical interpreters, between teachers as masters and students as clay to be "formed." According to this model, multidimensional critical exegetes remain masters of the text, even though this mastery of the text is now multidimensional rather than one-dimensional. They present themselves as masters—a source of great scandal for feminists and many other disciples ("little ones," Matt. 18:6), as I have discussed. Rather than being accountable to readers of the Bible who, in one way or another, are "other" than they, such multidimensional exegetes would despise these "others" and their otherness ("despise . . . little ones," Matt. 18:10). We can then draw a second conclusion.

> Conclusion 2: Appropriate multidimensional critical exegetical practices must be framed by a nonhierarchical conception of the relationship between critical and ordinary readers.[67] This is a conception (related to the model of a discipleship of equals) according to which the otherness of others is valued and affirmed, rather than despised and denied.

"Uncritical" Multidimensional Exegetical Practices: A Second Inappropriate Conception

I suspect that, for many of us male European-American exegetes, the preceding conclusion confirms that our resistance to the proposed multidimensional practice is well founded. We perceive such a proposal as a threat to our vocation as critical exegetes. Even when we acknowledge that the views advocated—(1) a text is multidimensional; (2) a given methodology focuses the interpretation upon one dimension; (3) critical exegeses are interested—are at least as plausible as alternate views, we are not convinced that they characterize our practices. We cling to our usual view of critical exegeses as one-dimensional disinterested practices because of our convictions that only these practices are in accord with our vocation as *critical* exegetes. Our resistance is rooted in our raison d'être; we *feel* that a conception of critical exegetical practices as multidimensional and interested threatens our sense of vocation.

The irony is that our very resistance in the name of our vocation provides another argument that should convince us to acknowledge that all critical exegeses are interested and thus that we should adopt a multidimensional critical practice. We resist the notion that critical exegeses are interested because such a notion is contrary to our commitments as critical exegetes, that is, contrary to the "interests" and "concerns" that, by vocation, we feel we must defend and address. This shows that our resistance is not so much to the basic principles enunciated above, but to an inappropriate form of multidimensional practice that would prevent our performing our task as critical exegetes.

This envisioned inappropriate form of multidimensional practice fuels our resistance to any such conception of exegetical practices because it would involve a renunciation of being "critical." In our effort to be ethically accountable to many different people who are directly or indirectly affected by our work, we would abdicate our ethical accountability to the Academy, which demands a rigorous respect of the text. Our resistance presupposes a multidimensional practice that, because it would emphasize the polysemy of any text and acknowledge the interested character of all critical interpretations, would reduce critical interpretations to the level of "uncritical" interpretations that distort the texts in an attempt to make them say what the interpreters want them to say. Any clear distinction between critical and ordinary readings would be abolished. Furthermore, since the envisioned multidimensional practice would involve the use of a plurality of critical methodologies and the selection and adaptation of critical methods for specific interpretive goals, critical methods would be reduced to the role of artifices for justifying any interpretation that the interpreter fancies. Critical interpretations would become nothing more than clever word games rather than serving to rigorously elucidate and establish the characteristics of a given text.

The resistance to this inappropriate form of multidimensional practice is quite legitimate. It shows in another way that we cannot hope to be accountable to those affected by our works if we (pretend to) abdicate our own cultural identities, interests, and concerns—including our vocation as critical exegetes—since in so doing, we would (pretend to) be disinterested and thus would continue to be androcentric and Eurocentric.

From this, we can draw a third conclusion.

Conclusion 3: An appropriate form of multidimensional exegetical practice must include the affirmation of our sense of vocation as "critical" exegetes as an integral part of our identities and interests.

More specifically, our resistance to multidimensional practices shows that our sense of vocation as critical exegetes requires this fourth conclusion.

> Conclusion 4: An appropriate form of multidimensional exegetical practice for us must (*a*) maintain a clear distinction between critical and ordinary readings and (*b*) pursue the elucidation and establishment of characteristics of a given text through the use of critical methods.

Envisioning Appropriate Multidimensional Exegetical Practices

The foregoing four conclusions are interrelated.

First, for most of us male European-American critical exegetes the question is this: Would multidimensional exegetical practices allow us to fulfill our vocation (conclusions 1 and 3)? So long as we identify our vocation with the one-dimensional practices through which we seek to fulfill it, we can envision only a negative answer to this question and would thus want to maintain our traditional one-dimensional practices. Yet as I argue in chapter 3, when we take time to reflect on our vocation (that is, to become self-conscious about our interests and concerns and to evaluate the effectiveness of our present practices for fulfilling this vocation), it becomes clear that (*a*) the effectiveness of our past and present one-dimensional practices is dubious and (*b*) androcritical multidimensional practices promise to be more effective ways of fulfilling our male European-American critical vocation.

Thus it is imperative that each of us make explicit our specific sense of vocation as a critical exegete in a specific context—and thereby the interests and concerns—that a multidimensional exegetical practice must fulfill. This is what I have done for myself: Chapter 3 clarifies the goals of critical biblical studies and the epistemological basis of the conception of criticism implied in my specific exegetical practice as a Protestant male European-American exegete. But instead of proposing a model of critical practices that should be adopted by everyone, chapter 3 invites other exegetes in a like manner to determine their own specific sense of critical exegetical practice.

A second question is this: How can one make a clear distinction between critical and ordinary readings (conclusion 4) without conceiving their relationship in a hierarchical way (conclusion 2)? I argue that this is possible only insofar as we recognize that (*a*) ordinary readings are basically legitimate; they account for actual features of the text; (*b*) this legitimacy of ordinary readings is due to the role of the text in the reading process; that is, the text has the power–authority of affecting readers in certain ways; and (*c*) critical readings are always based upon ordinary readings, and far from providing the basis for legitimate ordinary readings (the hierarchical conception), critical readings are based on the ordinary readings that they bring to critical understanding.

It is now clear that, once again, this has led us into unexpected territory. I began this chapter with the hope that a methodological solution could address the ethical problem of our lack of accountability. It is now apparent that my methodological proposal for a multidimensional critical exegesis is necessary but not alone sufficient, because in and of itself it might easily be inappropriately envisioned as maintaining a marked distinction between the critical and the ethical, viewed as being in a hierarchical relationship.

Envisioning appropriate multidimensional practices with the above characteristics involves a shift of other parts of the old paradigm, this time concerning the relationship between the ethical and the critical, and thus the relationship between our vocation (our commitment to do "what is good") and critical practices and the relationship among text, ordinary readings, and critical readings. From this perspective, the ethical is perceived as intrinsic to the critical. Because it entails a paradigm shift in order to show that the above suggestions are at least as plausible as our traditional presuppositions, rather than engage in a theoretical discussion, in chapter 3 I discuss these issues in terms of what has personally convinced me of their plausibility in my own experience as a Protestant male European-American critical exegete who seeks to acknowledge the *Protestant* context from which he speaks. In it I acknowledge the contextual character of my proposal for an androcritical multidimensional exegetical practice and thus make this proposal truly androcritical.

NOTES

1. In preparation for my *Discipleship according to the Sermon on the Mount: A Multidimensional Androcritical Exegesis* (Minneapolis: Fortress Press, forthcoming).

2. Biblical quotations are from the New Revised Standard Version, unless otherwise indicated.

3. For example, E. Schweizer, *The Good News according to Matthew* (Atlanta: John Knox Press, 1975), 432.

4. In this passage, the disciples are warned about "causing to stumble" or "scandalizing" (*skandalizein*) others.

5. Schüssler Fiorenza, *In Memory of Her*, 150–51.

6. Ibid., 140–51.

7. Georg Strecker, *The Sermon on the Mount: An Exegetical Commentary* (Nashville: Abingdon Press, 1988). See also idem, *Der Weg der Gerechtigkeit: Untersuchung zur Theologie des Matthaus* (Göttingen: Vandenhoeck and Ruprecht, 1962).

8. Ulrich Luz, *Matthew 1–7: A Commentary* (Minneapolis: Augsburg, 1989).

9. W. D. Davies and Dale C. Allison, Jr., *A Critical and Exegetical Commentary on the Gospel according to Saint Matthew* (Edinburgh: T&T Clark, 1988). See also, W. D. Davies, *The Setting of the Sermon on the Mount* (Cambridge: Cambridge University Press, 1964).

10. Hans Dieter Betz, *Essays On the Sermon on the Mount* (Philadelphia: Fortress Press, 1985), 17–36, and idem, *Synoptische Studien II* (Tübingen: J.C.B. Mohr, 1992), 219–89 (see also 92–110).

11. Schüssler Fiorenza, *In Memory of Her,* 153–54.

12. This "choice" of one of the two meaning-producing dimensions discussed here (among others that are not yet discussed) is a real "choice" only insofar as the different dimensions of the text are perceived as equally legitimate and equally valid (according to the text), a point discussed below. Note that this choice is made here on the basis of ethical considerations about our responsibility toward those affected by our work. It is a theological decision, as Schüssler Fiorenza underscores in her study, "The Twelve and Discipleship of Equals," in Schüssler Fiorenza, *Discipleship of Equals: A Critical Feminist Ekklesia-logy of Liberation* (New York: Crossroad, 1993), 104–16.

13. As long as they are not the "same" as their master, they cannot propose a legitimate interpretation. See once again the discussion of the different types of relation to the "other" in Dussel, *Philosophy of Liberation,* 16–66.

14. As discussed below and in chapter 3, another condition is that this multidimensional presentation be androcritical.

15. This is the very attitude that David Fisher challenged us to adopt in his 1986 response to D. Jobling's paper, "Deconstruction and the Political Exegesis of Biblical Texts: A Reading of Some Royal Psalms" (SBL Structuralism and Exegesis Section, 1986) by speaking of "the text and its masters," and later in "The Texts and Their Owners" (SBL Structuralism and Exegesis Section, 1987). This involves putting into question our proudest accomplishment as exegetes, mastering the text, which establishes our authority as teachers. See also Fisher, "Self in Text, Text in Self," *Poststructural Criticism and the Bible,* 137–54.

16. See also D. Patte and G. Phillips, *Teaching the Bible Otherwise: Can We Be Responsible and Critical in a Pluralistic Context?* (forthcoming).

17. This point is underscored in Richard A. Edwards, "Uncertain Faith: Matthew's Portrait of the Disciples," in *Discipleship in the New Testament,* Fernando F. Segovia, ed. (Philadelphia: Fortress Press, 1985), 47, who emphasized that we should not expect to find in Matthew "a unified view of the disciples."

18. The same could be said about the way in which semio-literary or sociological exegetical methods are most often practiced.

19. These comments do not apply in the same way to Schüssler Fiorenza's subsequent books, especially *But She Said: Feminist Practices of Biblical Interpretation* (Boston: Beacon Press, 1992), in which she emphasizes the plurality of practices in feminist biblical rhetorics of interpretation.

20. Of course, this is itself a methodology, and culturally conditioned.

21. This is also true of a deconstructionist methodology. Even though deconstructionists might prefer to speak of "deconstructionist anti-methodology," they presuppose an epistemology; consequently, their approach fits the definition of methodology

proposed above. For instance, "reading against the grain" ends up being perceived as an affirmation of the authority of this unconventional reading over against traditional readings, even though deconstructionists might not intend it in this way.

22. It is enough, for our present purpose, to contrast two methodologies and their respective views of "redaction." Redaction would be viewed in still other ways from the perspectives of methodologies based upon the social-sciences (sociology, anthropology, and/or psychology) and upon orality (methodologies that are underdeveloped and yet should play an essential role in "oral" cultures). For example, see, respectively, Bruce J. Malina and Richard L. Rohrbaugh, *Social-Science Commentary on the Synoptic Gospels* (Minneapolis: Fortress Press, 1992); and Werner H. Kelber, *The Oral and the Written Gospel: The Hermeneutics of Speaking and Writing in the Synoptic Tradition, Mark, Paul, and Q* (Philadelphia: Fortress Press, 1983).

23. This is the procedure that Bornkamm inaugurated and that he and his students used in a series of studies first published in German between 1948 and 1957, and published in English in Günther Bornkamm, Gerhard Barth, Heinz Joachim Held, *Tradition and Interpretation in Matthew* (Philadelphia: Westminster Press, 1963).

24. The shift from a historical to a semio-literary understanding of "redaction" already occurs in Perrin's latter works. See Norman Perrin, *Jesus and the Language of the Kingdom* (Philadelphia: Fortress Press, 1976). Even though literary studies (e.g., Mary Ann Tolbert, *Sowing the Gospel: Mark's World in Literary-Historical Perspective*, Minneapolis: Fortress Press, 1989) and semio-structural studies (such as my commentary on Matthew) do not identify themselves as "redaction critical studies," they have the same concern as historical redaction critical studies: establishing the "redactor's" point of view. Yet, from the perspective of semio-literary methodology "redaction" is now conceived of as a "discoursivization" process. See Patte, *Religious Dimensions*, 97–98, 173–202, 258–64.

25. Demonstrating this point would demand presenting a plurality of semio-literary exegeses of Matthew 23, something which I cannot do here. Yet, see my *The Gospel according to Matthew*, 321–23, which already expresses how the discipleship of equals is attributed to Matthew, and my *Discipleship according to the Sermon on the Mount*, for an example of multidimensional exegesis as applied to the Sermon on the Mount.

26. Similarly, Fred Burnett concludes that the significance of the proper name "Jesus" is undecidable in Matthew. See Fred W. Burnett, "The Undecidability of the Proper Name 'Jesus' in Matthew," in David Jobling and Stephen D. Moore, eds., *Poststructuralism as Exegesis*, Semeia 54, 123–44. My concern and that of Burnett and other poststructuralist scholars are similar, in that all of us seek to overcome the usual critical exegetical practices that view a text as "decidable."

27. From these comments, the main difference between my proposal for an andro-critical multidimensional exegesis and a poststructuralist exegesis (such as Burnett's; cf. n. 26, above) is discerned. While Burnett emphasizes the "undecidability" of the text, I emphasize the "pluri-decidability" of the text (due to its multidimensionality). My emphasis is rooted in the concern to account for the multiplicity of "ordinary readings" (and of critical readings), each of which has "decided" in favor of one or another dimension of the text.

28. Rudolph Bultmann, "Is Exegesis without Presuppositions Possible?" in *Existence and Faith: Shorter Writings of Rudolph Bultmann* (Cleveland: World Publishing Company, 1960), 289–96.

29. Of course, in other works, and for different but related purposes, Schüssler Fiorenza develops other kinds of methodological approaches: a critical rhetorical paradigm in *Bread Not Stone: The Challenge of Feminist Biblical Interpretation* (Boston: Beacon Press, 1986); a literary-functional approach in *Revelation: Vision of a Just World* (Minneapolis: Fortress Press, 1991); an interdisciplinary feminist critical theory in *But She Said: Feminist Practices of Biblical Interpretation.*

30. This is a point that is already made, although in a different form, in Walter Wink, *The Bible in Human Transformation: Toward a New Paradigm for Biblical Study* (Philadelphia: Fortress Press, 1973).

31. To avoid any confusion, I need to specify that "interested," "interests," "concerns," and "group" are, for me, technical terms that I understand against the background of a semiotic theory of interpretation and reading—more specifically, a theoretical model concerning "enunciative contract" and "social semiosis." In brief, the interests and concerns of an interpreter are never his or hers own alone but actually that of a "group." This "group" is a social entity, which might eventually become institutionalized. But it is first of all defined as a "discourse space"; persons participate in this group by virtue of sharing a common kind of discourse. They abide by a certain discourse-interpretation contract characterized by a "morality of knowledge" and "codes" (embodied in methodologies and methods) through which they protect or address the interests and concerns of the group. This theoretical view is a formulation in terms of Greimas's semiotics (see A. J. Greimas and J. Courtés, *Semiotics and Language: An Analytical Dictionary*) of the analysis of "social semiosis" by Jürgen Habermas, *Knowledge and Human Interest* (Boston: Beacon Press, 1971), already largely expressed by Mieke Bal, *Femmes imaginaires. L'Ancien Testament au risque d'une narratologie critique* (Paris: Nizet, 1986). For a convenient summary, see Mieke Bal's discussion of "codes" in *Murder and Difference*, 3–11. Yet in this book, I do not seek to develop a theoretical argument to justify this view. What convinced me of the validity of this theoretical view was, ultimately, the concrete questions directed to me regarding my critical practices as a male European-American exegete: It required a paradigm shift.

32. For me, a given methodology is "contextual" in that it reflects a certain cultural situation. As such, it reflects the interests and concerns of the dominant group in that cultural situation. Yet I keep the qualification "interested" for the specific critical exegeses, because the exegetical practices reflect the more specific interests and concerns of subgroups in the given cultural situation. Thus, for instance, the historical-critical methodology and its methods (which reflect Eurocentric interests and concerns in a certain period) are used by male European-American exegetes in an androcentric perspective, as well as by certain feminist exegetes such as Schüssler Fiorenza.

33. The clear-cut distinction between hermeneutics and exegesis underscored by K. Stendahl, "Biblical Theology, Contemporary," *Interpreter's Dictionary of the Bible*, 1: 418–32.

34. Feminists and other proponents of advocacy hermeneutics (along with deconstructionists and reader-response critics) might be disappointed that I do not write, "The traditional distinction between critical exegesis and hermeneutics *is abolished.*" As I understand them, they refuse any distinction between critical exe-

gesis and hermeneutics, so as to emphasize that the former has no less an advocacy or interested character than the latter (e.g., Schüssler Fiorenza, *In Memory of Her*, 35 and *passim*). I agree. I also reject the subject-object dichotomy and the particular distinction between exegesis and hermeneutics *in terms of "what it meant" and "what it means."* Yet adopting a position beyond the subject-object dichotomy does not mean rejecting the distinction between critical and precritical ordinary readings. I believe it is useful to maintain a distinction between two kinds of advocacy interpretations for which the traditional terms "critical exegesis" and "hermeneutics" are good designations. There are "aspects of reference" in text that can be described, even though in an "interested" way. See Bernard C. Lategan and Willem S. Vorster, *Text and Reality: Aspects of Reference in Biblical Text* (Philadelphia: Fortress Press; Atlanta: Scholars Press, 1985). Further reasons for maintaining this distinction are explained in chapter 3, below.

35. This is a point I discuss in greater detail in "Textual Constraints, Ordinary Readings, and Critical Exegeses: An Androcritical Perspective," in *Textual Determinacy: Part 1. Semeia* 62 (Atlanta: Scholars Press, 1993), 59–79.

36. Amy-Jill Levine, *The Social and Ethnic Dimension of Matthean Salvation History* (Lewiston, N.Y.: Edwin Mellen Press, 1988), minimizes it by underscoring that those who are condemned are "people in positions of leadership," whether they are Jews or not. While her interpretation is quite convincing, it remains that the text still conveys anti-Judaism to its readers.

37. Amy-Jill Levine, "Matthew, " in Newsom and Ringe, eds., *Women's Bible Commentary*, 252–62, and Patte (*The Gospel according to Matthew*) minimize both the anti-Judaism and the patriarchalism conveyed by Matthew.

38. For instance, Samuel Sandmel, *Anti-Semitism in the New Testament?* (Philadelphia: Fortress Press, 1978); and Michael J. Cook, "Confronting New Testament Attitudes on Jews and Judaism: Four Jewish Perspectives," in *The Chicago Theological Seminary Register*, Vol. 77, no. 1 (winter 1988). See also Fred W. Burnett, "Exposing the Anti-Jewish Ideology of Matthew's Implied Author: The Characterization of God as Father," *Ideological Criticism of Biblical Texts, Semeia* 59 (Atlanta: Scholars Press, 1993), 155–91.

39. For instance, Schüssler Fiorenza, *In Memory of Her*.

40. These dimensions are related to those discussed earlier. A discipleship of equals would be consistent with discipleship as servanthood and also with loving one's enemies. Similarly, an authoritarian-patriarchal discipleship would be consistent with the patriarchal character of the Gospel as a whole and also with anti-Judaism. Thus, one can suspect that the conflicting interpretations could be explained by differences in methodologies and methods (possibly, variations of the same method focused in different ways by different methodological epistemologies).

41. See Burnett, "Exposing the Anti-Jewish Ideology of Matthew's Implied Author," and his bibliography therein. Note that against his argument of his previous article about "The Undecidability of the Proper Name 'Jesus' in Matthew," here Burnett presupposes the *decidability* of Matthew's ideology. I want to argue that this ideology is as undecidable as any other meaning-producing dimensions of Matthew.

42. Schüssler Fiorenza, *Bread Not Stone*, xiii; a comment she makes about the Bible as a whole.

43. Philip P. Hallie, *Lest Innocent Blood Be Shed: The Story of the Village of Le Chambon and How Goodness Happened There* (New York: Harper & Row, 1979).

44. We, European-American male exegetes, cannot any longer ignore such advocacy interpretations. They are not a fad that will pass, while "true" critical exegesis will endure. One does not need to be a prophet to predict that the present advocacy biblical studies are nothing but the vanguard of a multitude of such studies.

45. This is still an important aspect of the task of critical interpretations for Bultmann (*Existence and Faith*, 289–90), although it is no longer the primary one for him—over against the views of other exegetes whom he refers to in notes.

46. Albert Schweitzer, *The Quest of the Historical Jesus: A Critical Study of Its Progress from Reimarus to Wrede* (New York: Macmillan Co., 1968).

47. Ernst Troeltsch, "Historiography," in James Hastings, ed., *Encyclopedia of Religion and Ethics* (New York: Charles Scribner's Sons, 1914), 6:716–23. See also his recently republished essays in *Religion in History: Essays* (Minneapolis: Fortress Press, 1991).

48. Hans Georg Gadamer, *Truth and Method* (New York: Seabury Press, 1975).

49. See Gadamer, *Truth and Method*, 235–305.

50. As Tracy says, summarizing an important aspect of Gadamer's proposal. See Robert M. Grant and David Tracy, *A Short History of the Interpretation of the Bible* (Philadelphia: Fortress Press, 1984), 159–60 (see 153–66); Gadamer, *Truth and Method*, 91–150.

51. What Gadamer also calls "effective-historical consciousness" (Gadamer, *Truth and Method*, xix; see 305–41).

52. A point I developed in different ways in Patte, *Paul's Faith*, 3–6, and *Religious Dimensions*, 6–10.

53. As is emphasized by Mary Ann Tolbert, when she writes: "One should select the method of study (in the case of biblical texts, the particular exegetical method, either historical or literary), first, on the basis of what one is seeking generally to learn from the text and, second, on the basis of the special aspects, circumstances, and characteristics making up the particular text under study" (*Sowing the Gospel*, 4; see also pp. 10–13, her "criteria for adjudicating interpretations"). Beyond Tolbert, I want to underscore that this statement is also a description of the way we use methods (and not merely a prescription).

54. Note that in these examples (and those that follow) I do not limit the groups to members of the Academy. While scholars might be the only ones to use these methods, they do so in the service of the interests and concerns of many others who directly or indirectly benefit from the exegetical works and thus tacitly find these methods appropriate.

55. For instance, both Strecker and Luz express that their respective interpretations address the needs, interests, and concerns of certain of their liberal contemporaries: for Strecker, the needs of the church under the threat of a nuclear holocaust and confronted by the Peace Movement ("the Greens"; cf. Strecker, *Sermon*, 22–23; 181–85); for Luz, the needs of pastors and priests who, in the modern,

busy world, are at risk of a "premature burnout" (Luz, *Matthew 1*, 9, 95–99). Yet according to them, this does not mean that their choice of a specific method, their specific implementation of it, and their respective interpretations are influenced in any way by their desire to address the concerns and interests of this specific group. It just happens that the text addresses them when it is interpreted in a totally disinterested way.

56. A point discussed at length in Patte, *The Religious Dimensions of Biblical Texts*, 5–12 and passim. See also Robert G. Hamerton-Kelly, *Sacred Violence: Paul's Hermeneutic of the Cross* (Minneapolis: Fortress Press, 1992), 1–9 (his explanation of his use of René Girard's theory, rather than another theory). This view of theory is shared by scientists, especially those involved in fundamental research. Indeed, as C. Baglin, a nuclear physicist, emphasized in explaining his work to me, scientific theoretical research would be pointless with any other view of theory. It is this view of theory that Kuhn presupposes in his discussion of paradigm shifts. See Thomas Kuhn, *The Structure of Scientific Revolutions*.

57. In science, this is the case, for instance, of the several and quite different theories about the electric phenomenon that are used for different concrete uses of electricity.

58. The following argument is a brief summary of my discussion of the relations between historical and semio-literary critical methods in D. Patte, *Religious Dimensions*, 1–17, passim.

59. This pragmatic acknowledgment is manifested by the inclusion of these diverse methods and methodologies in the program of learned societies, by their publication in referred journals or book series, by the acceptance of expertise in different methods as ground for academic promotion, and the like.

60. See Van Harvey, *The Historian and the Believer*, 68ff.

61. As defined by J. Elull, *The Technological Society* (New York: Vintage Books, 1967).

62. See Strecker, *Sermon on the Mount*.

63. See Ulrich Luz, *Matthew 1–7: A Commentary*.

64. A point underscored by Mieke Bal in *Murder and Difference*, 3–11, passim, where she emphasizes the role of "codes" (subsuming the interests and concerns of a group) in interpretation.

65. See again, Schüssler Fiorenza, "The Ethics of Interpretation: De-Centering Biblical Scholarship."

66. As feminist, womanist, and mujerista scholars showed to me at the Vanderbilt conference, "Ethical Responsibilities and Practices in Biblical Criticism," in March 1991, sponsored by the Lilly Endowment Inc.

67. Note that the contrast is no longer between "critical and uncritical" readers (which implies a negative judgment of the latter), but between "critical and ordinary" readers.

3. A Quest for Accountability: Androcritical Exegetical Practices

In chapter 2, I noted that the suspicion of feminist and advocacy scholars and the resistance of male European-American exegetes forced me to recognize that multidimensional critical exegetical practices, while necessary, are not a panacea that will automatically make our practices ethically accountable both to the Academy and to those affected by our work as male European-American exegetes. In order to be ethically accountable, multidimensional critical exegetical practices must acknowledge their interested character and, as a consequence, must recognize that critical readings and ordinary readings (which are usually explicitly "interested") belong together—rather than in a hierarchical relationship. In sum, our practices must be androcritical.

While these conclusions seemed to be sensible and logical responses to the aforementioned suspicion and resistance, their significance for an understanding of critical exegetical practices appeared to me only after I underwent a paradigm shift about other important aspects of critical exegetical practices.

In order to recognize the interested character of our critical practices, it is essential to have a clear view of the relationship between our vocation as critical exegetes and our critical practices. But to do this, we must first undergo a paradigm shift on this issue. While feminist and other advocacy scholars readily make explicit their vocation—the goals of their interpretations—we, male European-American critical exegetes, underscore our critical practices and the methodological issues (as I did in chapter 2) because we simply assume that our vocation and our practices are closely attuned to each other. This assumption was dispelled as soon as I examined the relationship between my vocation and my actual practices. By adopting this androcritical perspective, I recognized not only the interested character of my exegetical practices but also additional problematic features of one-dimensional exegetical practices, which clarified for me why they cannot help but be ethically irresponsible.

Similarly, we must undergo a paradigm shift regarding the relationship between ordinary and critical readers in order to conceive of them in a nonhierarchical way. Until then, we will spontaneously envision this relationship as hierarchical and cannot even imagine it in any other way. Yet a nonhierarchical relationship between ordinary and critical readers can be envisioned when one respects the claims of ordinary readers that the text has the power-authority to affect them. Without denying the important role of readers in the reading process, one is then in a position of recognizing that authentic ordinary readings— that is, those that truly reflect how readers have been affected by a text—must be viewed as basically legitimate, in the sense that they reflect actual features of the text. Once this is acknowledged, it becomes clear that the legitimacy of an ordinary reading does not depend upon a critical reading—the relationship is *not* hierarchical.

The following question, then, must be raised: If the distinctive task of critical exegetical readings is not to legitimate ordinary readings (which, from this perspective, would be illegitimate on their own), what is it? In this new light, I can only conclude that *the goal of critical exegesis is the bringing to critical understanding of an ordinary reading*. According to this androcritical definition, a critical reading should not be envisioned as a negative assessment of ordinary readings, but as the elucidation of the actual features of the text (and its context) that are reflected by ordinary readings. In this light it will become clear that accountability in critical exegetical practices involves the affirmation of the otherness of the others and of their interpretations.

These conclusions are not a prescription, asking us to do something new or different. They are a description of what we are already doing, albeit selectively, in our exegetical practices, when we bring to critical understanding our own ordinary readings (hunches, insights, theses). I simply suggest that our task should include helping other people bring to critical understanding their own ordinary readings. Furthermore, since such ordinary readings are often *faith*-interpretations, the critical exegetical task can be understood as a *theological* one: It is the bringing to critical understanding of faith-interpretations (a paraphrase of Anselm's *"fides quaerens intellectum"*). In view of the diversity of potentially legitimate ordinary readings to be brought to critical understanding, only a multidimensional critical exegesis can carry out this task.

Such are the points I underscore in this chapter, which is divided into three distinct sections. As in the previous chapters, I begin by sharing how the requisite paradigm shift happened to me in the very process of writing this book.

Section 1.
Vocation and Practices of a Protestant Male European-American Critical Exegete

My Vocation as a Critical Exegete

Before moving to the personal, it is fitting to ask the broader question: Why do we feel it is urgent and important for us to provide critical interpretations of biblical texts—so much so that we devote our lives to this task? The general answer, which subsumes a diversity of more specific answers, is clear: because we are convinced that "uncritical" interpretations of the Bible have devastating effects.

Acknowledging My Sense of Vocation as a Critical Exegete

Although we rarely make it explicit, I think it is fair to say that our sense of vocation is still rooted in the Enlightenment.[1] From this perspective, the critical exegete's vocation is to free people from their obscurantist readings of the Bible (be they dogmatic, evangelical fundamentalist, or integrist). This is a responsibility we feel we must assume, because of the damaging psychological, social, political, cultural, and/or religious effects of such obscurantisms—damaging effects that are different forms of alienation[2] of other people.

As a Protestant male European-American critical exegete, my sense of vocation takes three different forms that, without excluding one another, have different emphases. These three forms correspond to successive stages of my career as a critical exegete.

1. For me, as for most Protestant male European-American exegetes, critical exegeses are explicitly or implicitly developed in order to counter evangelical fundamentalist interpretations,[3] or, more constructively, to provide alternative critical readings that displace these uncritical readings.[4] As is well known, many of us are former fundamentalists who had firsthand experience with the legalistic and stultifying fundamentalist interpretations (as we see them now, after our liberation from them through critical studies) that alienate individuals and engender or justify patriarchal, paternalistic, patronizing (if not

racist), anti-Jewish (if not anti-Semitic) behaviors both in the churches
and in society. Our sense of vocation is basically defined by our concerns to overcome these fundamentalist interpretations and their
disastrous alienating consequences through critical studies that acknowledge the complexity of the biblical texts due to their historicity.

2. Our sense of vocation is further defined for some of us (especially
in secularized Europe) by our concerns for a no less disastrous and
alienating effect of obscurantism, namely, dechristianization, or secularization. Fundamentalist interpretations of the Bible (as well as other
kinds of dogmatic interpretations, such as integrist ones) make it impossible for modern people to appropriate the biblical message and
thus are a cause of secularization and of the dehumanization that ac-
companies it. In this case, our sense of vocation is defined by our concerns to overcome the historical gulf that separates modern people
from the Bible and that obscurantist interpretations deepen by ignoring it. This is what we hope to achieve by our critical studies of the
Bible, as part of a hermeneutical project (e.g., Bultmann's demytholo-
gization project) that would elucidate both the historicity of the biblical texts and that of their interpreters and readers.

3. Our sense of vocation is further redefined for others of us who
were nourished by the ecumenical movement: Our primary concerns
are for another disastrous and alienating effect of obscurantism,
namely sectarianism, and the resulting church divisions. Fundamentalist and other dogmatic interpretations of the Bible fuel exclusivistic attitudes through the claim that they propose "the" only legitimate and
valid meaning of the Bible ("the biblical message"). On the basis of this
claim, fundamentalist interpreters reject and exclude Christians who
have beliefs and interpretations of the Bible different than theirs, viewing them as hypocritical or perverted. This sectarian attitude engenders or justifies similar exclusionary attitudes in society (e.g., viewing
other people as less than human, in the same way that other Christians
are viewed as less than Christian).[5] Here, our sense of vocation is defined by our concerns to overcome these obscurantist interpretations
and their consequences through critical studies that elucidate the diversity of biblical beliefs and messages.

The sense of vocation in any of the above variants is all the more in-
cumbent upon us because evangelical fundamentalist readings of the
Bible also have the paradoxical effect of transforming into a means of
alienation a book, the Bible, which in our view is in itself essentially liberating. Thus our vocation also includes freeing the Bible from obscurantist interpretations. For many of us, this exegetical task must be
carried out for the sake of the church, even as we confront the churches
and their uses of the Bible.

I can recognize my own sense of vocation in each of the above three variants. Although my practices are more directly governed by the third one, the others are still very much present with me.

Affirming the Legitimacy and Validity of My Sense of Vocation

I can readily affirm the legitimacy and validity of my particular sense of vocation, as well as of the more general anti-obscurantist vocation and the specific forms it takes for non-Protestant male European-American critical exegetes. This sense of vocation is "legitimate," because it addresses actual situations, the reality of which we Protestant male European-American critical exegetes cannot deny, since they are part of our undeniable experience.

It is "valid" (has a positive value) because it is an expression of our concern to address an actual problem: fundamentalism (and more generally, obscurantism) and its negative consequences. Our vocation is an ethical resolve to overcome the moral scandal resulting from those fundamentalist interpretations that find, for example, in Matthew a legitimation for ecclesial and social patriarchy, for subtle and not so subtle anti-Judaism and even anti-Semitism, for stultifying and enslaving religious moralism and legalism, for individualistic piety that condones and reinforces existing social injustice by ignoring its many forms, for secularization and its dehumanizing consequences, and/or for sectarianism.

Our vocation also includes a sense of ethical responsibility for the quality of life and social justice in those societies in which we are in leadership positions. Of course, in the process, we secure our position of power. We do not need to apologize for this—any more than feminist and other advocacy scholars need to apologize for seeking power for themselves and their own groups—although in view of our history of misuse of power, we need to be especially careful to avoid conceiving this power as exclusive. So, this anti-obscurantist vocation must include a commitment to sharing power with those who are excluded by fundamentalist interpretations on the basis of their different religious tradition, social status, gender, or race.

When we misuse our power (for instance, by our implicit or explicit elitist claim that only educated people can have the right kind of interpretation of the Bible), we actually betray our vocation, for under the pretense of fighting against obscurantist oppression, we promote classism, a similar kind of oppression. Conversely, striving to be effective in fulfilling our vocation must also involve striving to use power for liberation rather than for oppression.

Acknowledging and Affirming Others' Sense of Vocation

We Protestants readily join forces with other male European-American critical exegetes who perceive their vocation similarly. Thus our sense of vocation has a "male" and "European-American" character. It finds expression in the identification of the basic human predicament as "obscurantism," which most often we Protestants perceive theologically as a form of idolatry: absolutizing what is not absolute. Then our very vocation demands that we acknowledge that our own views are not absolute. Our identification of the basic human predicament is contextual in that it reflects our own experience and specific perception of what is problematic in religious, social, political, and cultural practices around us. Consequently, we can affirm the legitimacy and validity of our identification of the basic human predicament and of our sense of vocation (overcoming this predicament), but only if we do not absolutize this identification of the basic human predicament and our sense of vocation.

It follows that, in order to be consistent with our own sense of vocation as male European-American critical exegetes, we should also affirm the legitimacy and validity of other views of vocation of critical biblical scholars—for example, those of feminist and other advocacy biblical scholars—that are grounded in different views of the basic human predicament that reflect their different contextual experiences and specific perceptions of what is problematic. In sum, our own sense of vocation requires that we affirm the *legitimacy* of the different views of vocation of most other interpreters of the Bible.[6] Yet we have to contest the *validity* of any vocation that claims to be the only legitimate and valid one.[7]

These observations raise a surprising question: Does not our sense of vocation demand that we acknowledge the legitimacy of the evangelical fundamentalists' different sense of vocation, even as we contest its validity because of its sectarian character?

Before I address this issue, the primary conclusion of the preceding discussion needs to be underscored: We, Protestant male European-American exegetes, can and should affirm the legitimacy and validity of our specific sense of vocation and carry it out. Then the most immediate questions are: How are our present (one-dimensional) critical exegetical practices implementing this vocation? With what results? Since, as it soon appears, the efficiency of our current practices is dubious, the question becomes: Why is this the case? What *critical* exegetical practices would be more efficient ways for fulfilling this vocation?

The Dubious Effectiveness
of One-Dimensional Practices

Are We Succeeding in Overcoming
the Disastrous Effects of Fundamentalism?

Our one-dimensional critical exegetical practices had much success. The people freed from their fundamentalist obscurantism through our teaching are legion. Our publications directly or indirectly (e.g., through preachers) contribute to the positive transformation of many others.

Yet there are numerous signals that these successes are accompanied by dubious consequences and results. I noted in chapter 1 the negative effects of our work on Jews, women, African-Americans, and other Christians from cultural contexts different from ours. Another signal that our one-dimensional practices are not as effective as we hoped is that, far from succeeding in bringing about at least a reduction of fundamentalism, they have been unable to prevent its growth. In the U.S., evangelical fundamentalists were once properly called a "silent majority." They have since become more vocal. In secularized Europe, churches with fundamentalist leanings seem to be the only ones truly alive. In Central and South Americas, as well as in Africa and Asia, fundamentalist or fundamentalist-like churches are on the rise.[8]

Our Questionable Assessment of the Problem
Represented by Evangelical Fundamentalist Interpretations

These general observations are enough to show that our traditional one-dimensional critical exegetical practices are not an efficient means of fulfilling our vocation. An examination of the way in which we, Protestant male European-American one-dimensional critical exegetes, traditionally deal with evangelical fundamentalists and their literalistic biblical interpretations—a "family dispute," since evangelical fundamentalists are themselves Protestant—clarifies the basic problem that plagues our practices. It shows that even as we seek to reverse key features of evangelical fundamentalist interpretations, we keep in our exegetical practices the same basic pattern that characterizes those interpretations.

So how do we challenge evangelical fundamentalist interpretations through one-dimensional practices? By denying any legitimacy to these interpretations because they allegedly do not respect the text. By claiming that these are "uncritical" readings that betray "the" meaning of the text as established by our critical exegeses: for example, "what the text meant" (in its original historical context), or more recently, "the literary meaning of the text" (as defined by one or another semio-literary critical method).

As we see it, the problem is that evangelical fundamentalists read into the text their religious preunderstandings, making it say what they want to hear, and hide their betrayal of the text by appealing to the authority of the text as sacred scripture, Word of God. Armed with our critical methodologies (which, for all intents and purposes, we perceive as collectively freeing us from preunderstandings; see chapter 2), as critical exegetes we profess to be guardians and protectors of the text— as if the text was powerless to protect itself, and as if we had the power-authority to control what constitutes legitimate interpretations of the text.[9]

In our zeal to overcome the disastrous consequences of fundamentalist interpretations—the uncritical character of which is hidden by appeal to the authority of the biblical text—do we usurp the power-authority of the text? We, at any rate, deny power-authority to the text. We practice critical exegesis, as if the root problem with evangelical fundamentalist interpretations were that undue and excessive authority—indeed, divine authority—is attributed to the biblical text.

This implicit analysis embodied in our practices seems adequate, even though we also affirm that this appeal to the authority of the text is a smoke screen hiding a betrayal of the text. Is it not the case that for evangelical fundamentalists the text has so much authority as divine revelation that it has meaning in and of itself and that it transcends any context? That the message of the gospel is "supracultural"?[10]

Consequently, in order to prevent fundamentalist interpretations, we emphasize that the actual meaning of the text can only be comprehended when one takes into account the context of its production— according to one's methodology and epistemology, either its historical context (including the author's intention) and its literary context (including its relations to traditions and other texts) or the context in which the text is read. As a result, we remove authority from the text; the locus of authority is displaced. Authority—authoritative meaning—is located somewhere "behind the text" or "in front the text,"[11] rather than "in the text."[12] Consequently, we, as critical exegetes who are equipped to assess what is "behind" or "in front" of the text, alone have the power-authority to control what constitutes legitimate interpretations of the text.

The results of our assault on what we take to be the premises of evangelical fundamentalist interpretations are, at best, ambivalent. On the one hand, fundamentalist interpreters continue to flourish by dismissing and ignoring critical exegeses and their "scandalous" denial of the authority of the Bible. On the other hand, exegetes-believers who have no tendency to be fundamentalists are in a dilemma.[13] They must either (1) deny their convictions about the authority of scripture (an integral component of their faith) and to divorce themselves from the community (church) gathered by this faith, in order to practice critical exegesis; or (2) adopt a fundamentalist interpretation of the Bible in order to preserve their convictions about the authority of scripture. As a consequence, ministers trained in critical exegesis too often revert to uncritical fundamentalist interpretations of the Bible, as one can verify by listening to their sermons. Then critical exegesis has failed to reach its goal. Worse, it actually promotes fundamentalist interpretations. Even in the successful instances when fundamentalist interpretations are prevented, the cost is very high. The scriptural authority of the biblical text is denied. Without its foundation the Christian community can only crumble or become another kind of faith community—a community characterized by "the strange silence of the Bible,"[14] a community "afraid of words."[15]

An Alternative Assessment of the Problem Represented by Evangelical Fundamentalist Interpretations

These observations once again underscore the dubious effectiveness of one-dimensional critical practices. Are our practices based on an inadequate analysis of the problem posed by obscurantist interpretations and their disastrous consequences? Is the attribution of excessive authority or power to the text the root problem with evangelical fundamentalist interpretations? Is their claim to respect the authority of the text insincere or even fraudulent? Is it the case that the evangelical fundamentalists' appeals to the authority of the text—by using "proof-texts"—are merely a way of justifying the projection of their preunderstandings upon the text?

Evangelical fundamentalist interpreters vehemently deny such accusations by critical exegetes.[16] It is true that when they claim absolute authority for the text they actually claim authority for their own interpretations and for themselves. From our perspective as outsiders, this is a usurpation of the authority of the text. Yet for them (as I remember from my perspective as a former insider), such an identification of the authority of the text with that of their interpretations is not problematic *because their affirmation of the authority of the text precedes their interpretations and provides a basis for them,* rather than being a deceptive afterthought (as we suspect it to be). Before proceeding to any systematic interpretation (tentative exegetical readings in biblical study groups and dogmatic readings), evangelicals are convinced that the biblical text has authority and power. Let us not forget that the faith of evangelicals is rooted in a personal experience in which the biblical text deeply affects and transforms them, and that they experience this transformation as a liberation from destructive sinful powers. This is what happens to them in their "devotional readings" (ordinary readings) and what they express in their "testimonies" when they narrate the way in which they were converted from their sinful lives. The power and authority of the biblical text is something that they have experienced and that they cannot deny.

Whatever might be this experience of the power-authority of the text, and whatever might be our evaluation of it, as critical exegetes we should not deny that people have such experiences. The biblical text is perceived by evangelicals as having power-authority over them. It is with this conviction that they proceed to interpret the biblical text. Yet we deny their experience through our one-dimensional practices, which presuppose that the basic problem with evangelical fundamentalist interpretations is their deceptive affirmation of the power-authority of the biblical text. Whether or not it is a self-deception does not make any difference in this assessment.[17]

The reasons for the failure of our one-dimensional critical practices to overcome fundamentalist interpretations and their disastrous consequences and thus in fulfilling our vocation are several. First, we demand from evangelical fundamentalists that they deny an experience that they cannot deny without abandoning their identity and their raison d'être: the transforming power of the biblical text. Consequently, most of them simply brush away our critical works and ignore them. Second, we fail to fulfill our vocation in a more basic way: Our one-dimensional practices, which are supposed to overcome the alienations resulting from fundamentalist interpretations, themselves alienate all evangelicals, whether they are fundamentalist or not. They affect evangelicals in the same way they affect women, African-Americans, and other people who are culturally or religiously different from us.

Third, in addition to duplicating the problematic consequences of the fundamentalist interpretations that they are supposed to overcome, one-dimensional practices also duplicate a characteristic of their dogmatic interpretations: their one-dimensionality. Indeed, their dogmatic statements make it clear that evangelical fundamentalists conceive of the text as a meaningful entity with a single meaning: "the" true meaning of the text; a universal and unchanging ("eternal") meaning; the "supracultural" message of the gospel inspired by God; the "fundamental" teaching of the text expressed in "propositional truths."[18]

Thus the root problem with fundamentalist, or dogmatic, interpretations is certainly similar to the one with one-dimensional critical practices. In light of our earlier discussion of these practices, I can draw two conclusions:

1. The root problem with evangelical fundamentalist interpretations (what makes them alienating) is *not* their evangelical affirmation of the power-authority of the biblical text in and of itself (as our one-dimensional critical practices presuppose), but rather their implicit claim that *the biblical text exerts its power-authority in a single way*—the way in which the fundamentalist interpreters have experienced it.

The root problem is a universalization of their experience with the text, and thus a form of androcentrism and/or Eurocentrism, which leads them to conceive their systematic interpretations as the one-dimensional establishment of *the* "fundamental propositional truth" of each biblical passage. In other words:

2. The disastrous consequences of fundamentalist interpretations do not result from the experience of the power-authority of the biblical text, but from the subsequent absolutization of this experience.

It is ultimately because we misapprehend the root problem with evangelical fundamentalist interpretations that we fail to fulfill our critical vocation and pursue one-dimensional critical practices. We need to envision our critical practices in terms of a proper understanding of this root problem, if we truly want to overcome the consequences of fundamentalist interpretations.

Section 2. Ordinary Reading and Critical Reading

Lessons from Evangelical Readers of the Bible

The practices that would fulfill our vocation as male European-American critical exegetes by overcoming the alienating effects of fundamentalist interpretations would avoid duplicating these effects. Our practices must not alienate others, including evangelical fundamentalists. The question is, How can we criticize evangelical fundamentalist interpretations and overcome their disastrous consequences without alienating evangelical fundamentalists? We can do it by affirming the basic legitimacy of their evangelical interpretations. An apparently paradoxical suggestion? Let us consider more closely the situation.

Affirming the Otherness of Others as a Part of Effective Critical Exegetical Practices

One of the problems in the total rejection of fundamentalists and their interpretations through our traditional one-dimensional critical practices is that we ignore that our conflict with them is a "family dispute." We should not forget that evangelical fundamentalist interpreters[19] are themselves Protestants who belong, with us, to a Eurocentric and androcentric culture. Totally rejecting them, their experience, and their interpretations amounts to denying—or better, pretending to deny—a part of our own identity and contextual perspective. To me, this is one of the main reasons for our betrayal of our own vocation and our inadvertent adoption of the most inappropriate feature of fundamentalist practices—their one-dimensionality.

In order to settle this "family dispute," we must acknowledge that we belong to the same "family," and thus that we have much in common. This process involves becoming self-conscious about the legitimate concerns and interests that we *share* with evangelical fundamentalists because all of us are participating in a Eurocentric and androcentric culture. Simultaneously, we also need to acknowledge that our "family" includes different members, with different (more specific) legitimate concerns and interests resulting from different kinds of experiences in special contextual situations. These two types of acknowledgment are, for me, necessary characteristics of what I call "androcritical" practices. As Protestant male European-American critical exegetes, we must simultaneously acknowledge what we share with evangelical fundamentalists and affirm the legitimacy of their different concerns, interests, and experiences. Contrary to our traditional polemical attitude, this amounts to acknowledging the legitimacy of basic features of their interpretations because we recognize in these features either the expression of legitimate concerns we share with evangelical fundamentalists or differences that we can affirm as legitimate.

Wheat and Weeds in Biblical Interpretation

This essential shift in attitude—adopting a positive attitude toward evangelical fundamentalists—does not mean that we renounce our vocation to overcome the disastrous alienating effects of fundamentalist interpretations, but rather that we seek to avoid duplicating these effects in our own practices. We are very much like the servants of the parable of the weeds among the wheat (Matt. 13:24–30). We are rightfully concerned by the presence of weeds in the wheat field of fundamentalist interpretations. But we are so concerned by the weeds that we exclusively envision their immediate uprooting; totally ignoring the wheat, we see only weeds. But as the householder expresses, this is precisely the wrong thing to do. Such a polemical practice of uprooting weeds would have an even more disastrous effect than the presence of the weeds in the field: It would result in the uprooting of the wheat. The appropriate practical response is one that is conceived in terms of the "positive features" of the situation: Indeed, the weeds need to be destroyed; but for the sake of the wheat, one has to be patient enough to wait for the proper time.[20]

In order to recognize that evangelical fundamentalist interpretations are a wheat field with weeds, and not merely a field of weeds, let us remember that our own one-dimensional practices as male European-American critical exegetes is also a wheat field with weeds—indeed, with similar weeds: the alienation of others through the absolutization of our own perspective. It is this observation that led me to the conclusion that the basic problem with fundamentalist interpretations is that they are absolutized; the evangelical experience of the power-authority of the biblical text is turned into dogmatic interpretations.

This conclusion includes a distinction between (1) the evangelical fundamentalists' experience of the power-authority of the biblical text (as believers read the Bible in their "ordinary readings"), and (2) the subsequent dogmatic interpretations that absolutize this experience. Denouncing these *dogmatic* interpretations as weeds does not require a similar rejection of the experience of the power-authority of the biblical text in an earlier reading. Indeed, it is quite possible that this experience (devotional or ordinary readings) is "wheat" and that the effort to more clearly understand these readings through systematic biblical studies with other believers (the "tentative exegetical readings" practiced in biblical study groups) is an expression of legitimate concerns and interests. The weeds would then be the ways in which this experience is publicly defended in dogmatic interpretations—a third kind of reading reflected in preachings, apologetics, and polemics. This appears when we consider more closely these three types of evangelical fundamentalist readings and their interrelations as first-level, second-level, and third-level readings, instead of exclusively focusing our attention upon the absolutizing fundamentalist interpretations (third-level, "dogmatic" readings), as we usually do.

Evangelical Ordinary Readings and "Faith-Interpretations" as Basically Legitimate

The experience of the power-authority of the biblical text occurs as evangelicals read (or hear) the Bible and are moved, transformed, and often liberated by it. This is a devotional reading, an "ordinary reading," which results in what I call a "faith-interpretation." At this point evangelical believers readily acknowledge that this is a very "personal" reading, a personal experience resulting in a personal faith-interpretation.

Such an ordinary reading does not make any universal or absolute claim. On the contrary, it acknowledges its devotional and thus intuitive character; it does not perceive itself as an authoritative interpretation. It also acknowledges its contextual, or personal, character: The biblical text affects believers in different ways in different situations. A given believer *does* claim that his or her specific faith-interpretation of a given biblical text is the only one that is truly valid for him or her at a specific time. It has transcendent value for him or her; it is God's Word for the believer in the present situation. Yet this believer does not claim that this faith-interpretation expresses the only legitimate and valid message of the text; he or she expects that its message (God's Word through this text) will be different in other circumstances. This capacity to speak an appropriate Word to different people in different places and times is, for evangelical believers, an intrinsic part of the power-authority of any biblical text.

Thus at this stage, neither the specific experiences of the power-authority of the biblical text in evangelical ordinary readings nor the resulting faith-interpretations are universalized. At the very least, they are not in and of themselves alienating; they do not demand that other people deny their own experiences and faith-interpretations. Furthermore, from the positive perspective advocated above, one can suspect that these experiences and faith-interpretations are legitimate; they reflect the way in which given aspects of the text have actually affected certain readers.

Before discussing the plausibility of this suggestion, and in order to recognize it, it is essential to avoid any confusion between these ordinary readings, or faith-interpretations and other readings, which are superimposed upon them: second-level and third-level readings. Fundamentalist dogmatic readings are third-level interpretations through which fundamentalists ultimately absolutize their evangelical faith-interpretations. Tentative exegetical readings are second-level interpretations that seek to make sense of, and to justify for oneself and others, one's ordinary readings and faith-interpretations. These are necessary and appropriate.

Evangelical Tentative Exegetical Readings as Basically Legitimate "Theological" Interpretations

The necessity of evangelical theological exegetical readings appears as soon as one considers the fragile status of ordinary readings. An ordinary reading (e.g., the reading of a novel) does not need to be justified to anybody else, as long as one's life is not significantly affected by it. But one is compelled to justify this ordinary reading when one's life is transformed by it: One needs to explain the changes in one's behavior to others. This is all the more true when these changes are religious in nature and thus concern one's entire life, as is the case with evangelical devotional readings and faith-interpretations of the Bible that bring about their conversion and sustain their faith: they establish the fundamentals of one's life as a believer.

Even though an evangelical faith is very personal, based as it is upon a personal experience of the power-authority of the biblical text, its legitimacy needs to be confirmed by others who had similar personal experiences. Because a faith includes a vision of the reality, meaning, and purpose of human life, "one cannot have faith by oneself,"[21] that is, it is very rare for one to hold a totally idiosyncratic faith that nobody else shares. If the legitimacy and validity of one's faith is not confirmed by at least some other people, either one abandons it (the most frequent cases) or one is alienated and is perceived as insane. For an evangelical, this means that his or her experience of the power-authority of the biblical text and faith-interpretations—the bases of his or her faith—need to be justified to at least some other people, and naturally, first of all to others who have the same type of experience and faith-interpretations. This is what happens in biblical study groups. An evangelical community of faith is established. Such a community is necessary so that evangelical faith might survive and flourish.

For evangelical believers, the *validity* of the experience of the power-authority of the biblical text and of the resulting faith-interpretations—that is, their positive value as that which determines the believers' ultimate concerns and interests[22]—is demonstrated by the very existence of the evangelical community of faith. A given evangelical believer is confirmed in his or her conviction that this experience brings about a positive transformation of his or her life by the fact that other members of the biblical study group had a similar reading experience and affirm its value. The value of this shared experience is expressed by the affirmation that the Bible is the "Word of God," a phrase that, for evangelicals, conveys (among other things) that the Bible has the power-authority of positively transforming the personal lives of believers.

The establishment of the *legitimacy* of the experience of the power-authority of the biblical text and of the resulting faith-interpretations is another matter. It demands that an evangelical demonstrate to the satisfaction of others that the biblical text has in fact the power-authority to communicate the message that the believer intuitively perceived in a devotional ordinary reading of a given passage, and that he or she adopted as his or her faith-interpretation. The nature of this demonstration appears when one takes note that the devotional reading is intuitive, in the sense that it is a reading that is performed without being self-conscious about the interpretation process involved. The believer simply "feels" that he or she is affected by the text in a certain way, and thus that the text means something (the faith-interpretation) that directly concerns him or her. The demonstration that the biblical text has in fact this power-authority involves, therefore, bringing to understanding how the text had such an effect. This is done through a self-conscious systematic study of the text and of its features aimed at verifying that this meaningful message is indeed what the text says. This evangelical systematic study is a theological interpretation, according to Anselm's definition of the theological task, "faith seeking understanding" (*fides quaerens intellectum*); it seeks to understand a faith-experience and the faith-interpretations of biblical texts that result from it.

Nevertheless, this theological systematic study has an objective character in that it seeks to establish that the meaning of a biblical text according to the faith-interpretation is truly grounded in what the text says. This is required by the nature of the evangelical faith-interpretations: It is based on an experience of the power-authority of the biblical text. This is also required so that others in the Bible study group (and beyond) who have different faith-interpretations (even though theirs are also based on an experience of the power-authority of the text) might acknowledge its legitimacy. Furthermore, this theological systematic study has a critical character, in that it often demands refinements of the faith-interpretation—refinements that might be quite drastic and include a rejection of certain features of the faith-interpretation. Thus it is appropriate to say that such theological systematic studies are exegetical interpretations, as evangelicals claim at times despite the protests of one-dimensional male European-American critical exegetes.

We protest because, to us, such theological systematic studies are not worthy of the title "exegeses" since they are uncritical. Is this not what evangelicals grant by acknowledging that their interpretations are grounded in the believers' faith-interpretations? This amounts to saying that their theological systematic studies are based on preunderstandings. Yet in light of my discussion of the role of preunderstandings in critical exegeses (see chapter 2), I have to conclude that this characteristic of evangelical exegeses cannot be a reason for rejecting them as illegitimate. They have as much potential for respecting the text as do our own critical exegeses, which are also grounded in preunderstandings.

Consequently, I want to argue from the positive perspective proposed above that even if these interpretations are different from ours, they should be considered legitimate until proven otherwise. They might simply be focused on a meaning-producing dimension of the text different from the one(s) on which our own critical studies are focused. In addition, since these theological exegeses are offered as justifications of certain faith-interpretations to other people who do not hold them, in order to be convincing they have to be consistent in their descriptions of the features of the text (a test of legitimacy, as we shall see). Thus at the outset, we can suspect that evangelical theological exegeses (and consequently the faith-interpretations they seek to justify and understand) are legitimate, even when they are affirmed by fundamentalists. Yet I want to go even further.

Evangelical Theological Interpretation as a Model for Androcritical Multidimensional Exegesis

The preceding observations suggest to me that this evangelical practice of theological exegesis is a model that we male European-American critical exegetes should emulate instead of rejecting without further examination. By this, I do not mean that we should adopt the evangelicals' preunderstandings or faith-interpretations. Our negative reactions to evangelical interpretations show that we no longer share their specific experiences of the power-authority of the text and thus their specific faith-interpretations. Nevertheless, we share something with evangelicals, whether they are fundamentalist or not. Like them, we interpret with preunderstandings, which are faith-interpretations in the general sense that they are precritical interpretations (ordinary readings) that appear to us as self-evidently true and reflect our ultimate concerns. Even if these precritical interpretations are secular, anti-religious, and negative readings of the Bible, they belong to the realm of faith, that is, to the realm of self-evident convictions and ultimate concerns.[23] It follows that instead of rejecting evangelical theological exegeses as presumably illegitimate, we should emulate them by making explicit the preunderstandings that are presupposed by our own exegeses. Indeed, we also should acknowledge that our own critical exegeses are theological, in that they bring to understanding our own faith-interpretations.

These surprising suggestions need to be further explained. Before doing so, I must underscore that I do not suggest that we should emulate fundamentalist dogmatic interpretations. The latter are easily confused with evangelical theological exegeses because they simply add to them another layer of interpretation and because they are the fundamentalist interpretations that we outsiders most commonly encounter.

Fundamentalist Dogmatic Interpretations
as Illegitimate and Obscurantist

Evangelical theological exegetical interpretations of a given biblical text in various Bible study groups are often quite different from each other. This is to be expected, since they bring to understanding a diversity of experiences of the power-authority of biblical texts and a diversity of faith-interpretations. Yet this situation poses a problem for evangelical fundamentalist communities which for dogmatic reasons envision themselves as gathered around a "fundamental" biblical truth—a series of propositional truths that form a coherent doctrine that reflects the unity of Scripture and its univocity as Word (singular) of God (who is One). Consequently, in order to be properly justified for such communities, theological exegetical interpretations must not only demonstrate that they are consistent interpretations of the text, but also that they are consistent with the fundamental doctrines of a given fundamentalist community. A new, dogmatic layer of interpretation (which can also be called ideological) is added.

Whether this additional test precedes or follows the theological exegetical interpretations, it transforms them into dogmatic interpretations. What is brought to understanding in the interpretations is no longer the diversity of personal experiences of the power-authority of the Bible of the believers, but the established fundamental truth that is supposed to be the common denominator of the personal experiences of believers.

Then any theological exegetical interpretation that diverges from this fundamental truth is excluded as illegitimate and invalid, whatever the accuracy and consistency of its representation of the text might be. Despite the textual evidence underscored by this theological exegetical interpretation and the experience of the believer, "It is well known that it is not what the text says!"

As a result, potentially legitimate theological-exegetical interpretations are either rejected or subverted and transformed into illegitimate interpretations that discard the textual evidence and its consistency.

Similarly, the believer has either to accept being excluded from this community or abandon the distinctiveness of his or her theological exegetical interpretation, as well as his or her experience of the power-authority of the text, his or her faith-interpretation, and thus his or her identity as a believer. The evangelical interpretations, as they become fundamentalist and dogmatic, have become exclusive, sectarian, oppressive.

It is these fundamentalist dogmatic interpretations that our vocation calls us, male European-American critical exegetes, to reject. It is these dogmatic interpretations that have the disastrous effects that we are committed to overcome.

Ironically, the very claim of universality that makes these fundamentalist dogmatic interpretations alienating and unacceptable to us is what we emulate in our own one-dimensional critical exegeses, as we seek to counter them by proposing "the" only true critical interpretation. We should not be surprised when feminist and other advocacy scholars then denounce the lack of ethical accountability of our universalizing one-dimensional exegetical critical practices.

Furthermore, we should not be surprised that our one-dimensional practices that reject all evangelical fundamentalist interpretations so as to promote the only true critical interpretation would have a dubious effectiveness. Rather than merely questioning the dogmatic character of their interpretations, we demand from evangelical fundamentalists that they deny what they cannot deny without losing their identities as believers: their experiences of the power-authority of the biblical text, their faith-interpretations, their tentative theological and exegetical interpretations. Thus, our one-dimensional critical practices are not only ethically problematic but also ineffective.

Affirming the Basic Legitimacy of Evangelical Fundamentalist Interpretations

In order to fulfill our vocation to overcome the alienating effects of fundamentalist interpretations, we simply should not and cannot duplicate the problematic aspects of fundamentalist dogmatic interpretations: their absolutization and universalization of a given interpretation, the denial of the legitimacy of a plurality of interpretations, and ultimately, against its own basic convictions, the denial of the legitimacy of a plurality of experiences of the power-authority of the biblical text. This means that, in order to fulfill our vocation, we should acknowledge the legitimacy of a plurality of interpretations, rather than seeking the only true critical interpretation. We should recognize the presence of wheat in the fields, rather than being obsessed by the weeds. We should affirm the basic legitimacy of evangelical fundamentalist interpretations, even if it is somewhat hidden under alienating dogmatic reinterpretations.

This proposal, which at first seems surprising, is now clear. Evangelical fundamentalist interpretations, which in most instances take the form of dogmatic interpretations, are a wheat field with weeds; despite the presence of problematic features (weeds), which seem prevalent, they are basically good (wheat). Their dogmatic, alienating character is due to a subversive transformation of (potentially) legitimate evangelical theological exegeses, themselves justifications of (potentially) legitimate faith-interpretations based upon (potentially) legitimate experiences of the power-authority of biblical texts. In other words, the basis of alienating fundamentalist dogmatic interpretations—theological exegeses, faith-interpretations, and ultimately experiences of the power-authority of biblical texts—is something that our critical practices should affirm as legitimate.

If our critical practices could affirm this legitimacy without reservation (that is, if the parenthetical use of the word "potentially" in the above paragraph were removed), they would become very effective arguments against alienating fundamentalist dogmatic interpretations. They would show evangelical fundamentalists that by imposing a dogmatic test upon interpretations they themselves deny the very foundation of their own evangelical faith: They deny personal experiences of the power-authority of the Bible (which are different in different situations); indeed they deny the power-authority of the Bible itself (which includes the power to address the Word in different words to different people). Thus our practices would call evangelical fundamentalists to be faithful to their own basic convictions. Is there any doubt that such practices would be more effective in overcoming dogmatic interpretations than our present one-dimensional practices?

Furthermore, such critical exegetical practices would also satisfy the conditions for ethical accountability that we male European-American critical exegetes must implement in our exegetical practices: (1) We would acknowledge the specific contextual character of our own critical interpretations by affirming, rather than denying, their complex (both positive and negative) relationship with evangelical fundamentalist interpretations—a part of what it means to be *androcritical*. (2) We would conceive of the relationship of our critical interpretations with noncritical interpretations—ordinary readings and their theological justifications—in a nonhierarchical way, since we would recognize that critical interpretations make explicit the legitimacy that ordinary readings already have. (3) This kind of critical practice would truly be *critical* (in accordance with our vocation as critical exegetes) precisely because following evangelical fundamentalists, it would affirm the power-authority of the biblical text in the process of interpretation.

Yet most male European-American exegetes would not be convinced by such an appeal to evangelical fundamentalist experiences. For them, the question remains: Is it truly plausible to affirm the legitimacy of the evangelical fundamentalists' experiences of the power-authority of biblical texts? Similarly, is it truly plausible to affirm the legitimacy of the evangelical faith-interpretations and theological exegetical interpretations based upon these experiences?

Thus before outlining the more concrete features of the androcritical multidimensional exegesis that I propose in chapter 4 as one possible kind of ethically responsible exegetical practice, I need to show that it is indeed plausible in terms of recent theoretical discussions. More specifically, I need to show the plausibility of conceiving of critical exegetical practices that account for (1) the power-authority of the text in the reading process, and (2) the positive relationship between critical and ordinary readings. My point is that in the pluralistic cultural situation in which we male European-Americans live (whether we like it or not), this view of critical exegetical practices and of their relationship to ordinary readings are at least as plausible as traditional views are.

The Multidimensional Power-Authority of the Text in Ordinary Readings and Critical Readings

Acknowledging the Power-Authority of the Biblical Text: What Is at Stake?

Affirming that the power-authority of the text plays a significant role in the reading process amounts to affirming the legitimacy of evangelical fundamentalist experiences. What is at stake in this affirmation is the legitimacy of ordinary readings (as processes) and of the experiences of the power-authority of texts that they include, whoever might be the ordinary readers and whatever might be the texts.

By raising this issue, I question the traditional presumption that ordinary readings are illegitimate or uncritical. Some might be illegitimate (I allude to the case of "fake" readings, when one pretends to be affected by the text), but most are not, and thus they should be presumed to be legitimate until proven otherwise. Similarly, I do not suggest that we should recognize the evangelical type of experiences of the power-authority of the biblical text as the only legitimate one. Rather, I propose to acknowledge and affirm the legitimacy of a plurality of evangelical experiences of the power-authority of the biblical text, alongside that of a plurality of different experiences of the power-authority of the text by other people.

By advocating such recognitions and acknowledgments, I question the denial of the power-authority of the biblical text by many male European-American critical exegetes. Positively, I affirm that ordinary readings are as legitimate as critical readings; ordinary readings and critical readings are in a nonhierarchical relationship. Critical readings do make explicit (bring to critical understanding) the legitimacy of ordinary readings and in the process refine them; but conversely, ordinary readings (as expressions of ways in which texts actually affect people) are the source of the legitimacy of critical readings. Without ordinary readings as their bases, critical readings would be artificial word-games, and thus illegitimate.[24] But in order to perceive clearly the plausibility of this view, we need to recognize the plausibility of the view of the power-authority of the text affirmed by evangelicals, including fundamentalists.

In sum, I want to argue in this section that we (Protestant) male European-American critical exegetes should acknowledge the plausibility of the evangelicals' views according to which (1) the biblical text has power-authority to affect and transform its ordinary readers, and (2) ordinary readers in different situations are affected in different ways by this text. These views should be plausible for us, because they reflect an experience that we share with evangelicals: our experience as ordinary readers in a readerly culture (in contrast with oral cultures) of being mesmerized or fascinated by a text and of being positively or negatively affected by it.

Text as "Meaning Container" or Text as "Weaving"?

Raising the issue of the power-authority of a text is simply considering the role of the text in the reading process and thus in its relationship to the role of the readers, who are another locus of power-authority in the reading process.

With reader-response critics and many other European-American critics (including post-Bultmannian exegetes, specialists of hermeneutical theories, literary critics, semioticians, and poststructuralists), I conceive the reading process as an *event* through which meaning is produced as a result of the interaction between readers and text. From this perspective, a text in and of itself does not "have" meaning (is not "meaningful"); a text[25] offers "potentialities of meaning" that can be actualized in a reading process that makes the text "meaningful."[26]

Thus I have excluded the root metaphor according to which evangelical fundamentalists conceive the power-authority of the text in their dogmatic interpretations and that we also adopt too often in our one-dimensional critical practices (at times, against our theoretical views): the root metaphor of text as a "meaning container." It is true that this conception is supported by our frequent statements about the "meaning of the text" and about "meaningful texts." But such statements are common sense, post-facto explanations of our experiences, which should not be confused with our actual experiences as ordinary readers. Ordinary readings as processes are characterized by spontaneity and absence of self-consciousness about the reading process. Thus rejecting the image of text as meaning container is questioning not the legitimacy of ordinary readings, but one of their explanations. Actually, this metaphor misrepresents ordinary readings and their fluidity. As David Miller says, "From the perspective of this image, texts would be . . . carrying fixed meanings[27] within their walls, centered and secure, as on a potter's wheel. Texts—on this view—have their power in their content, in what they contain."[28]

Conversely, I have implicitly adopted another root metaphor: "text as weaving." According to Miller, "In this perspective, . . . the power of a text, including the Biblical one, would be in the patterns of its fabric, as in a tapestry, a design which can shape a life meaningfully and one in which a person or a people can be trapped, as in a web or net."[29] This dynamic metaphor of weaving is a more appropriate representation of the text in the varied experiences of the power-authority of the biblical text of evangelicals and other ordinary readers than the static metaphor of a container.

Extrinsic or Intrinsic Power-Authority of the Text? Both!

From the perspective of the weaving metaphor, following Miller, we need to take note that the power-authority of a text can be understood in different ways. It can be primarily located either outside or inside the text, according to what is privileged: the warp or the woof.[30] The question is: What is the place of the power-authority of the text (as weaving) in ordinary reading processes? There are two possibilities. (1) The power-authority of the text might be perceived as a *result* of the reading process; it would then be *extrinsic* to the text. Or, (2) the power-authority of the text might *precede* the reading process; it would then be *intrinsic* to the text. Both of these possibilities are plausible. Indeed, they should not be viewed as exclusive of each other, but as complementary—warp *and* woof.

The first possibility—the extrinsic power of the text—is based upon the presupposition that the power-authority of the text is tied to its meaning(s): It is through its meaning(s) that a text affects readers. Since meaning results from a reading process, one has to conclude that it is the text-as-already-read (and not the text in and of itself) that has power-authority. Readers attribute power-authority to the text. Readers and their contextually defined preunderstandings have a predominant role in the reading process. The text in itself is an inert and powerless object that is brought back to life and empowered by the readers.

This view is supported by the clearly contextual character of the various doctrines of biblical authority through the centuries as well as by the establishment of the canon of scripture: It is for reasons extrinsic to the texts (for instance, the orthodox churches' polemics against gnostic churches) that one book was ascribed scriptural authority and another was excluded from the canon. It is further supported by our feeling as readers that we are in control of the reading process. Is it not the case that the text is nothing but an inert thing on paper, that we can choose to read or not to read, to continue reading or to stop reading? Are we not giving power to the text by activating this otherwise inert object? Are we not attributing or denying authority to the text by accepting or refusing to submit to it? Furthermore, is it not the case that, depending upon the context from which we read, we produce out of the text a great variety of meanings and that our perception of the power-authority of the text varies accordingly? And so it is.

I cannot deny that extrinsic power-authority is ascribed by readers to certain texts because of the meanings associated with them as a result of certain readings. It is therefore plausible to conclude that we readers are the weavers who produce the "design which can shape a life meaningfully" or the "web or net" in which one can be trapped, as Miller says. Or, according to Ricoeur, we as readers of a "discourse fixed in writing" (a text) also occupy the place of the absent author; our reading is the weaving (or reweaving)—"a new writing, a writing in one's own words of what is written in the words of the text"[31]—which has the power-authority that a live discourse would have. This view is indeed plausible.

But I want to affirm that an alternate view is at least as plausible as this one, namely, the view that beside the extrinsic power-authority eventually attributed to it, a text also has an *intrinsic power-authority* that plays an essential role in the reading process.

This second possibility is based upon the presupposition that *the power-authority of the text is independent from its meaning(s)*. Consequently, the power-authority of the text does not result from the reading process through which meaning is produced. Before any intervention of readers, the text has power-authority. This can be understood by noting that although a text is a "discourse fixed in writing" (Ricoeur), it nevertheless is "a semantic representation of a discourse" (Greimas) that keeps essential characteristics of the discourse. For instance, while the elocutionary and rhetorical forces of the discourse are subdued, they are not completely suppressed. Furthermore, by the very fact that it is fixed in writing, the text acquires other power features: At the very least, as fixed in writing, it imposes constraints upon the readers, but also more positively, as semantic representation of a discourse it decisively contributes to the production of meaning(s) in the reading process by offering to its readers potentialities of meaning that elicit and indeed summon responses from them.

Our Experience of the Power-Authority of Texts: The Illusion of Being in Control of the Reading Process

The essential point that the text imposes constraints on the reading process is confirmed by our experiences as readers. Is it not our common experience that as soon as we truly interact with any text in a reading process, we are affected by this text? The text demands a response from us even as we read it, that is, before we have envisioned its meaning for us. Readers are forced to react to the text, positively or negatively, with passion or indifference, with fascination and excitement or with boredom and weariness, with consent and submission or with rejection and rebellion. By the very fact that we react to the text, we are transformed by the text. This is clear in the case of a positive response to the text; we are influenced, instructed, and/or taught by it. This is also clear when we are angered, outraged, or infuriated by the text. And the same thing is also true when our response as readers is indifference, boredom, and weariness. After reading, we are no longer the same persons; we are now defined as persons who are indifferent, bored, and left weary by this specific text, its subject-matter, and/or the way it presents this subject-matter.

As soon as we choose to read a text, we enter a process that will necessarily result in our transformation, even if it is a minimal transformation. Is this not why we carefully select the texts we ask our students to read? We expect our students to be affected in different ways by different texts. Similarly, when we write, we carefully craft our texts because we expect that different texts will have different effects upon our readers. In sum, through the reading process a text affects its readers, while the text remains fixed and is not transformed.

Is this power-authority of the text over readers an illusion? What is truly affecting us? Is it not the meaning (even if it is a partial meaning) that we produced with the text in the reading process or that we presupposed the text has, because we always read a text-already-read? Possibly. This is why I do not deny that extrinsic power-authority is ascribed to the text. Yet it is plausible to say that believing we are in total control of the reading process is an illusion. Actually, I think that one of the ways in which the text exerts its power over us is by fostering this illusion.

We male European-American critical exegetes commonly presuppose that we are in control of a reading process in which the text is passive when we strive to be self-conscious about our role in this process, for instance, by using critical methods and justifying their use. Such presuppositions are plausible, based as they are on the strong evidence of the readers' role. Yet they fail to raise seriously the issue of the role and power-authority of the text—especially, the power of a classic such as the Bible. Forgotten, ignored, suppressed, the power-authority of the text can exert itself in complete freedom upon us as critical readers; we confuse the effects of the text upon us with our interpretive abilities.

This confusion is illustrated by the objections (especially Ricoeur's) to Gadamer's proposal that the reading process should be viewed as a kind of dialogue with the text, a "game of conversation."[32] Even though Gadamer recognizes that the reading process is not a normal kind of dialogue, he insists that readers are not in control of it: We cannot play any game, including the game of conversation, while remaining self-conscious about what we are doing; we have to let go and allow the text to claim our attention by raising questions for us. Ricoeur objects that this is overlooking the distanciation that exists between writing and reading and between (absent) writer and (present) readers.[33] This distanciation implied by the text as "discourse fixed in writing" is the very condition of interpretation[34] (a point which, for Ricoeur, is essential for establishing the possibility of critical readings). Does not this distanciation put us readers in control of the reading process?

This seems to be the case. We initiate the reading process. Furthermore, because the text does not provide us with a prepackaged meaning-content, we readers cannot be passive recipients. We have to be producers of meaning because the text always offers itself as a puzzle that needs to be resolved by organizing its many pieces into a coherent picture—the coherent meaning of the text. This meaning does not exist as such; it needs to be put together. Since the reading process is the production of a coherent meaning out of a text that offers multiple possibilities of coherences, we critical readers are all the more convinced that we are in control of this process.

Fascinated by our own interpretive prowess, we forget that the text claims our attention, teaches us, moves us, convinces us, empowers us, or degrades us. We are oblivious to the fact that this particular text with its particular constraints affects us and has power upon us.[35] The more we are confident of being in control of the text (for instance, as an object that we analyze in critical studies) or of the reading process, the more we submit to constraints of the text. Yes, we do initiate the reading process. But in so doing we give life back to the inert text on the page, which now takes charge by claiming our attention and calling for responses to the issues that it raises. We readers cannot but respond and react to what the text proposes to us. Because it is written, fixed on pages, the text constantly remains in control, in a position of power; it keeps the initiative, it sets the subject matter of our dialogue.

The Multiplicity of Interpretations and the
Multidimensional Power-Authority of the Text

It is true that the meaning of the text is not prepackaged. We produce with a given text a great variety of meanings, which reflect our preunderstandings and our contextual situations. The multiplicity of interpretations of a given text once again seems to be clear evidence that readers have the primary role in the reading process. Yet, without denying the role of readers (these various meanings of the text are not prepackaged), it is plausible to conceive *the text as responsible for the multiplicity of interpretations*. For this, it is enough to keep in mind the polysemic character of any text and the plausibility of conceiving it as multidimensional (as I argued in chapter 2). The text does not offer itself as a simple, one-dimensional puzzle, but rather as a complex, multidimensional puzzle, the pieces of which can be organized into several different coherent pictures—several different coherent meanings of the polysemic text. We readers participate in the production of these "meanings of the text." But we do not make them up at will. We seize upon one of the several coherent meaning-producing dimensions offered by the text, or better, a dimension seizes us.

Because of our concerns and interests, one of these dimensions appeals to us, fascinates us, charms us. It captivates our attention so much that we do not see anything else in the text: It is this dimension that moves us, convinces us, or angers us, and out of which we ultimately produce *the* meaning of the text for us. Such is the power-authority of the text over us—a diversified, multidimensional power-authority that affects us all the more because we experience it in quite different ways in different situations and are thus convinced that we are in control of the reading process.

In sum, it is quite plausible for us, male European-American critical exegetes, to acknowledge that any text (including biblical texts) has a multidimensional power-authority over its readers. We can do so without denying the role of readers as important contributors to the production of meaning through the reading process; speaking about the power-authority of the text is simply acknowledging the role of the text beside the role of readers in the reading process.

It is therefore quite plausible for us to affirm the legitimacy of the evangelicals' experiences of the power-authority of the biblical text in their ordinary readings, rather than denying it as we implicitly do through our critical practices. Indeed, as I argued above, we Protestant male European-American exegetes should envision critical practices that embody such an affirmation if we want to develop critical exegeses that would truly fulfill our vocation. This acknowledgment of the multidimensional power-authority of the biblical texts is a necessary first step toward bridging the gap that separates our practices from our vocation; it brings about a reorientation of our attitude toward evangelical fundamentalists.

Yet this is not sufficient; as I have suggested, we also need to acknowledge the legitimacy of the evangelicals' faith-interpretations or ordinary readings.

Section 3. Critical Exegesis and the Affirmation of the Legitimacy of Ordinary Readings

The plausibility of affirming the legitimacy of evangelical faith-interpretations is best assessed by considering, on the basis of the above discussions (in this chapter and chapter 2), (1) the theoretical possibility of the legitimacy of any ordinary reading, and, in this light, (2) the relationship between ordinary readings and critical readings.

Ordinary readings or faith-interpretations are outcomes of a spontaneous and intuitive reading process. Ordinary readers are not self-conscious about the reading process and make no conscious effort to control it. Each such ordinary reading is an expression of the meaning of the text for (a) given reader(s) in a specific time and place: a *pro me* interpretation. Consequently, ordinary readers do not make any universal claims about their readings. At least implicitly, they acknowledge the contextual character of their ordinary readings that reflects their interests and concerns (preunderstandings), and thus their role in the production of these meanings with the text. In addition, ordinary readings reflect the power-authority that the text has exerted upon the readers. If it is true that a reader's interests and concerns focus his or her attention on a specific meaning-producing dimension of the text and especially if it is true that the text exerts its power-authority over the reader through one or another of its dimensions, the ordinary reading resulting from such a process should be *an appropriate representation of that dimension of the text* because of the role of the constraints of the dimension in the production of meaning—and thus should be legitimate. It follows that (1) when encountering an ordinary reading, we should presume that it is legitimate until proven otherwise; (2) critical exegetical studies should demonstrate that most ordinary readings are legitimate; and consequently (3) it is highly probable that evangelical faith-interpretations are themselves legitimate.

Critical Exegesis as Demonstrating
the Legitimacy of Ordinary Readings

The difficulty with the above theoretical conclusions is that they seem to be disproved by the fact that in most instances critical exegetical studies appear to demonstrate that ordinary readings are illegitimate. But before rejecting these conclusions, we should consider more closely our own practices. Are we correct in denouncing ordinary readings as illegitimate? And are we actually showing that they are illegitimate?

As I argued in chapter 2, we, male European-American critical exegetes, read the text with preunderstandings, as ordinary readers do; our critical readings are interested. The critical methods we choose to use and our implementations of them embody our preunderstandings and interests as members of specific groups. There is nothing problematic with this: Interested critical readings can be seen as critical, and thus as legitimate, when it is recognized that a text is multidimensional and that each given critical reading represents one of the meaning-producing dimensions of the text (the one that interests the critical reader).

A problem arises, however, when critical readings are one-dimensional, that is, when they pretend to represent *the* only true legitimate reading of a text, and thus when they deny their interested character. Such one-dimensional practices (mis)lead us into rejecting as illegitimate any reading, be it critical[36] or ordinary, that is governed by other interests and concerns. In other words, many of our rejections of ordinary readings as illegitimate are actually rejections of the interests and concerns that govern these readings. This is not a judgment about legitimacy. This is a judgment about *validity*, that is, about the value of being interested in one meaning-producing dimension of the text rather than another. In sum, when a clear distinction is maintained between *legitimacy* and *validity*, it appears that contrary to what seemed to be the case and to our claims, in many instances critical readings do not demonstrate the illegitimacy of the ordinary readings they reject.

Beyond this negative conclusion, I want to argue that far from suspecting all ordinary readings of being illegitimate, most *critical exegetical practices presuppose from the outset the legitimacy of certain ordinary readings*, namely, those of the exegetes. We are rarely aware of this, because our androcentric and Eurocentric critical practices do so surreptitiously, unlike advocacy critical practices that do it openly. The plausibility of this proposal appears when one considers the relationship between critical and ordinary readings.

Critical and Ordinary Readings
in Our Exegetical Practices

Critical readings have in common with ordinary readings the fact that they reflect the interests, concerns, and thus the preunderstandings of the readers, be they exegetes or ordinary readers. But critical readings are distinct from ordinary readings in that they are the outcomes of reading processes that are disciplined and controlled by the use of critical methods, instead of being spontaneous and intuitive. By contrast with ordinary reading processes, critical practices are self-conscious. This is at least what we male European-American critical exegetes claim, although the meaning of this claim is far from clear.

At first, it seems that speaking of self-consciousness regarding our critical practices is an overstatement. As critical readers we deliberately and thus consciously use critical methods. Yet this does not mean that we are "self"-conscious about our role in the reading process. A critical practice remains a reading process, that is, according to Gadamer, a game of conversation that readers cannot truly play as long as they remain self-conscious. Playing the interpretive game involves adopting a different consciousness—a role that we play and that is defined by both the critical method we use and the text. Thus it seems inappropriate to speak of *self*-consciousness.

Nevertheless, our deep sense that our critical practices are closely tied to our self-consciousness remains. First, as male European-American critical exegetes who have devoted our lives to this endeavor, we do not feel alienated as we practice our own kind of critical exegesis. Second, and more positively, our critical exegetical work gives us a sense of personal achievement and provides us with heightened self-understanding. Through our particular critical practice we elucidate something about the text that is quite significant for us because it expresses a truth that we recognize as something we obscurely held to be true all along. In other words, our critical practice reveals to us a truth that we held as self-evident and, consequently, a truth of which we were not conscious. It brings to consciousness some of our convictions (i.e., truths we hold to be self-evident) that are directly related to our ultimate concerns and interests and find expression in our preunderstandings. In sum, a part of our "self"—some of our convictions, aspects of our ultimate concern—are revealed to us through our critical reading of a text. It is a process that heightens our self-consciousness.

More concretely, *a critical practice is a reading process that brings to critical understanding the exegete's preunderstanding of a text.* This preunderstanding is often polemical. For instance, we male European-American critical exegetes intuitively feel in a precritical way that an interpretation is inadequate, misleading, or even erroneous, and thus we intuitively feel that an alternate interpretation that we at least dimly envision is appropriate and true. Our critical exegetical practice is a process through which we proceed to show with the help of critical methods that this intuitively felt alternate interpretation is legitimate, that is, demonstrably grounded in the text.

This formulation shows that the preunderstanding of the text that we bring to critical understanding is nothing but an ordinary reading: It results from a spontaneous and intuitive reading process, that is, from an ordinary reading process comparable to that of other ordinary readers. Certainly, our ordinary readings are different from those of other readers because they arise in the academic context[37] out of reflections on the history of interpretation of a given biblical text—instead of arising, for instance, in the present context of a community of faith in relation to personal devotion or to the struggle for social justice. But they remain ordinary readings, that is, intuitive, precritical readings.

Of course, we critical exegetes are not satisfied with such intuitive readings, which are amorphous, vague, and leave many gaps. Consequently, we quickly undertake to transform our ordinary readings into rigorous, clear, and systematic exegetical readings—so quickly that we forget that our exegeses originated in intuitive ordinary readings.

Critical Exegesis as the Bringing to Critical Understanding of Ordinary Readings

Thus we can conclude that through our critical practices we male European-American critical exegetes establish the legitimacy of our ordinary readings of the text. The only difference between our critical practices and, on the one hand, those of advocacy critical interpreters and, on the other hand, those of evangelicals in biblical study groups is that we conceal from ourselves and from others that our practices strive to establish the legitimacy of our ordinary readings.

We do this because our actual practices are at odds with our conception of the goal of these practices, a rift not unrelated to the rift between our vocation and practices discussed above. As critical exegetes, we are supposed to assess the legitimacy of ordinary readings. This is what we do by either affirming or rejecting the legitimacy of *other people's* readings. But we do not do so for our own ordinary readings—even if we pretend to do it by rejecting some aspects of our preunderstandings. In fact, *our critical exegeses rarely, if ever, fail to establish the basic legitimacy of our ordinary readings.* Our exegetical hesitations and the corrections we make in our critical studies of a text do not invalidate this point. Unless our ordinary readings have changed over time (a possibility, since they are contextual, in which case the critical process needs to start again), our hesitations and corrections are nothing but refinements of some aspects of our ordinary readings—ordinary readings are ever in need of improvements—or refinements of the arguments through which we seek to demonstrate the legitimacy of our ordinary readings.

In order to understand how it happens that we almost invariably show the legitimacy of our own ordinary readings, it is enough to remember that our ordinary readings are amorphous, vague, fleeting, intuitive, precritical interpretations. Through our critical practices, we give form to them, flesh them out, clarify them, anchor them into the text by making explicit references to the text's features and its historical and/or literary contexts, and bring them to critical understanding. Our use of critical methods is not really aimed at assessing the legitimacy of our ordinary readings in order to either affirm or reject them. Rather, we presuppose their legitimacy and strive to elucidate it and sharpen it. For this, each of us selects a critical method that will be adequate for bringing to critical understanding our own intuitive ordinary reading of the text (conceived as "the point we want to make" about the text) and implements this method in the way most suitable for this purpose.[38]

I do not suggest that this critical practice is inappropriate. We should not be ashamed of presupposing from the outset that our ordinary readings are legitimate. In so doing, we simply show our confidence in our own ordinary readings. This is quite proper, provided we do not transform this confidence into a boastful self-confidence by unduly attributing the successes of our ordinary readings to our own interpretive skills.[39] Our ordinary readings are, by definition, precritical. They do not depend on any of our exegetical skills; they precede them. Our ordinary readings remain intuitive perceptions of the appropriateness of certain interpretations of the text, as any ordinary reading is, even when they are polemically evoked by the reading of critical interpretations. Thus we cannot ground our confidence that our ordinary readings are legitimate in any special skill that we have as critical exegetes. This confidence *can* be grounded, however, in the decisive role of the text and its power-authority in any ordinary reading process. Having confidence in our ordinary readings is ultimately having confidence in the text and its power-authority. In effect, our traditional critical practices assume that because the text has such a power-authority over us as readers, our ordinary readings are in most instances legitimate, in that they properly reflect one or another of the meaning-producing dimensions of the text. Thus our initial presupposition that our ordinary readings are legitimate is quite appropriate.

The problem is that we conceal from the outset our presupposition that our ordinary readings are legitimate and that our critical exegeses are based on ordinary readings that we bring to critical understanding. We pretend to proceed to a disinterested study; through it, as we like to say, "we discover the meaning of the text." In so doing, we deny the actual character of our own critical interpretations. We deceive ourselves. We use double standards in our critical practices by presuming that our own ordinary readings are legitimate and that all other ordinary readings are illegitimate.

As a consequence of this rift in our practices, we betray our vocation even as we strive to fulfill it. We adopt an obscurantist attitude toward our own interpretations even as we strive to overcome obscurantism. We alienate others by universalizing our ordinary readings even as we seek to overcome the alienating character of fundamentalist interpretations. We become idolaters who oppress and destroy others, even as we are committed to struggle for justice. The root of the ethical problem with our critical practices appears in a sharper light: While presupposing that our own ordinary readings are legitimate, we presuppose that other people's ordinary readings are illegitimate.

As soon as it is exposed, it is clear that this double standard cannot be justified in any way. If our own ordinary readings can be presumed to be legitimate, the ordinary readings of other people, including evangelical fundamentalists and anybody else, must also be presumed to be legitimate. Each of these diverse ordinary readings has to be viewed as the representation of one or another meaning-producing dimension through which the text exerts its power-authority over certain readers who focus their attention upon this dimension rather than upon another because of their specific interests and concerns that reflect specific contexts.

Section 4. Conclusions

What can we, Protestant male European-American exegetes, learn from this androcritical examination of our work as critical exegetes?

First, we learn that we can only fulfill our vocation as critical exegetes and be ethically responsible if we envision our critical practices from the vantage point of a conception of multiple ordinary readings as legitimate reflections of the multidimensional power-authority of the text over its readers.

Second, by recognizing that any critical exegesis is implicitly or explicitly the bringing to critical understanding of an ordinary reading, making explicit the legitimacy that this ordinary reading already has, we put ourselves in a position of perceiving in a positive way the relationship among different critical interpretations as well as the relationship among ordinary and critical readings. A diversity of legitimate interpretations is expected. No interpretation can be rejected at the outset as illegitimate, even if it is very different from any recognized reading. Yet one must verify that this is an actual reading of the text (the way in which the text actually affects a reader), rather than a "fake reading" (students pretending to have read the text, even though they did not open the book).

Third, the orientation of our practice of critical exegesis needs to be reversed. In order to fulfill our vocation, we should not practice exegesis in order to exclude uncritical ordinary readings, but rather in order to demonstrate the legitimacy of the various ordinary readings of a text. The challenge for critical exegetes is to find the appropriate critical methodologies and methods—even if one has to develop them—which will make it explicit that these ordinary readings are in fact the result of how certain people in a specific context have indeed been affected by certain dimensions of the text.

Consequently, the collective goal of our critical exegetical practices should be to bring to critical understanding as many of the ordinary readings of the Bible as we can find. A great diversity of them is to be expected in the increasingly pluralistic and global culture in which we live. This means that each critical exegete would have the task of helping to bring to critical understanding not only her or his own ordinary reading, but also the ordinary readings of other people—especially those of people who are not trained as critical readers. To do so, two conditions must be met:[40]

1. We must have a clear awareness of our own status as critical exegetes. We do not attribute legitimacy to these ordinary readings. Our task is merely that of facilitators who help ordinary readers make explicit the legitimacy that their ordinary readings already have. These ordinary readers have produced by themselves a "correct," or legitimate, reading and they are already convinced of its legitimacy. Indeed, because of their different contextual settings, they reveal to us a legitimate reading that we would have never perceived without their help. Thus we are genuinely learning from them. Our role is merely to empower these ordinary readers to argue for the legitimacy of their own readings beyond their own group, namely, in the broader culture where academic warrants are in some sense perceived as authoritative. This entails teaching them how to recognize and affirm the distinctiveness of their own reading. (Note that there is no elitism in this perspective, in contrast with a view by which critical scholars ascribe the label "legitimate" or "illegitimate" to ordinary readings according to

their conformity or lack of conformity with the critical interpretation that serves as a benchmark.)

2. We must acknowledge that each of our critical exegetical interpretations is itself the bringing to critical understanding of an ordinary reading, whether or not this critical interpretation is performed with this awareness. For us male European-American exegetes, who are so used to making universal claims about our interpretations, this acknowledgment is possible only if we adopt an androcritical perspective and proceed to an androcritical multidimensional exegesis, which makes explicit that the existing critical interpretations of the Bible are indeed the bringing to critical understanding of ordinary readings that reflect the interests and concerns of our own group. Then, and then only, will we be in a position to acknowledge that other people's very different readings are as legitimate as ours.

We can thus conclude that our critical exegetical practices should ideally affirm the otherness of other people and their interpretations by bringing to critical understanding these interpretations. Whether it is or is not acknowledged, critical practices are always intrinsically ethical; they always include some kind of attitude toward the other, which affects all aspects of these critical practices. By being multidimensional and androcritical, that is, by being self-consciously a process through which a diversity of ordinary readings are brought to critical understanding, the critical practices of male European-American exegetes promise to be ethically accountable both toward the Academy and toward the many ordinary readers of the Bible around us. But we still need to understand how this promise might eventually be fulfilled. Chapter 4 will address this issue.

NOTES

1. Yet it is rooted in "a very anorexic version of the critical principle" (which is the Enlightenment ideal), as Edward Farley underscores in *The Fragility of Knowledge: Theological Education in the Church and the University* (Minneapolis: Fortress Press, 1988), 12; see 3–16. Despite a different focus, my comments go in the same direction. There is nothing wrong with our sense of vocation rooted in the Enlightenment and its "major correctives" (Farley's terminology); the problem is that this vocation is improperly practiced (i.e., that these correctives have been marginalized); it has become anorexic through ineffective practices.

2. Since "alienation" refers to "psychological, social, political, cultural, and/or religious effects," this term is used here and below in a broad sense that potentially encompasses several theories about alienation.

3. I use the phrase "fundamentalist interpretations" as we usually use it in order to refer to all kinds of fundamentalist evangelical interpretations, without making the many distinctions that are made in the evangelical camp among different

groups and their interpretations, such as the distinctions in terms of the views regarding inspiration of scripture among, for instance, "detailed" and "irenic in-
errantists" and "complete" and "partial infallibilists." See Robert K. Johnston,
Evangelicals at an Impasse: Biblical Authority in Practice (Atlanta: John Knox Press,
1979), 19–47.

4. Some biblical scholars make it explicit. For instance, see the work of James
Barr, which includes, besides many critical exegetical studies, books against fundamentalism such as *Fundamentalism* (Philadelphia: Westminster Press, 1978) and
The Scope and Authority of the Bible (Philadelphia: Westminster Press, 1980). The
concern that drives Barr in all his critical biblical studies becomes even more specific in *Biblical Faith and Natural Theology: The Gifford Lectures for 1991* (Oxford:
Clarendon Press, 1993): his concern for the negative effects of Karl Barth's and his
followers' "high" doctrine of scripture.

5. For examples described by a scholar who resolutely identified himself as an
evangelical, see Johnston, *Evangelicals at an Impasse*, 1–14.

6. In the same way, according to my interpretation of Galatians, Paul affirmed
the legitimacy and validity of different proclamations of the Gospel (a Gospel with
the law for the Jews and a Gospel without the law for Gentiles). Cf. Patte, *Paul's
Faith and the Power of the Gospel*, 39–85.

7. As Paul objected to the Judaizers. But the legitimacy of such absolutized vo-
cations is not contested, in the same way. In the case of the Judaizers, Paul did not
contest the "Gospel with the law" that they proclaimed to Jews, but only the claim
that this form of the Gospel was to be proclaimed to everyone, including Gentiles.

8. As was documented by the 1992 PBS television programs, *The Glory and the
Power: Fundamentalisms Observed*.

9. Of course, we would not dare to make such a claim for ourselves as individuals. But our way of practicing critical exegesis shows that we at least implicitly feel
justified to do so as a community of scholars because of the cumulative critical wisdom of several generations of scholars.

10. David J. Hesselgrave and Edward Rommen open their book *Contextualization: Meanings, Methods, and Models* (Leicester, England: Apollos, 1989) with these
words: "The missionary's ultimate goal in communication has always been to present the supracultural message of the gospel in culturally relevant terms" (1; see also
197–257). For them, *the* true meaning of a text is "supracultural"; it is a "revealed"
message.

11. During the last one hundred and fifty years of critical exegesis, this locus of
authority has changed several times. Since literalistic interpretations unduly identify Matthew's text with the words of the historical Jesus and view it as a factual
representation of his ministry, at first it readily made sense to say that the authority of the Gospel according to Matthew is located in the historical Jesus, rather
than in Matthew's text. Yet Albert Schweitzer, by his *The Quest of the Historical Jesus*,
inflicted on this quest for the historical Jesus a wound from which it will never
truly recover, despite the many attempts to keep it alive. The authority of the
Gospel was then located in the earliest strata of the tradition about Jesus (form
criticism), or in the development of the tradition as a normative process (cf. H.
Koester and J. Robinson, *Trajectories through Early Christianity* [Philadelphia:

Fortress Press, 1971]), or again in the theological and didactic intention of the redactor who seeks to address a specific church situation (redaction criticism, rhetorical criticisms and certain kinds of literary criticisms). With the advent of the semio-literary methodologies that emphasize the role of the readers in the production of meaning (reader response criticism in its various forms), the locus of authority has been situated "in front" of the text: the reading community. See, for instance, Edgar V. McKnight, *The Bible and the Reader: An Introduction to Literary Criticism* (Philadelphia: Fortress Press, 1985) and its bibliography, to which needs to be added works that bring together ideological criticism, rhetoric, and poetics, including: Meir Sternberg, *The Poetics of Biblical Narrative: Ideological Literature and the Drama of Reading* (Bloomington: Indiana University Press, 1987) and David Jobling and Tina Pippin, eds., *Ideological Criticism of Biblical Texts, Semeia* 59 (Atlanta: Scholars Press, 1993).

12. New criticism, formalism, and formalist structural criticism are the only methodological approaches that truly locate meaning-authority in the text and are rejected as inadequate by the proponents of other methodologies (including semiotics, the methodology that is the basis of structural exegesis). See, for instance, Patte, *Structural Exegesis*, and its bibliography.

13. This is the dilemma presented in great detail in the case of the historical-critical methodology by Van Harvey in *The Historian and the Believer*.

14. See James Smart, *The Strange Silence of the Bible in the Church* (Philadelphia: Westminster Press, 1970).

15. See the perceptive analysis of this situation by Gabriel Vahanian, in *Dieu anonyme ou la peur des mots* (Paris: Desclée de Brouwer, 1989). Vahanian underscores both the devastating effect on the church of refusing to be affected by words in general and by those of the biblical texts in particular, and the creative and transforming effect of submitting to the power of the text. This submission is a consequence of acknowledging that "Ce n'est pas le langage qui est, en effet, un instrument de l'homme, mais c'est l'homme qui est l'instrument du langage" (143). This statement can be paraphrased as follows (reversing McKnight's vocabulary in *The Bible and the Reader*): It is not the language that is an object that human beings manipulate (act upon and act with), but it is human beings who are the objects that language (the text) manipulates (acts upon and acts with). It is this power of language (the text) that the liberal churches (following the Western culture and male European-American critical exegetes) fear and attempt to escape by occulting it. See also Gabriel Vahanian, *L'utopie chrétienne* (Paris: Desclée de Brouwer, 1992), where the author underscores the verbal space of Christian utopia.

16. For a convenient summary of the objections of fundamentalists to the accusations of liberals and bibliography, see Richard J. Coleman, *Issues of Theological Warfare: Evangelicals and Liberals* (Grand Rapids: Wm. B. Eerdmans Publishing Co., 1972).

17. In effect, Dan Via expresses our basic assessment that fundamentalists deceive themselves (or have self-delusions) and our understanding of our vocation as the overcoming of such destructive self-deceptions when he writes in conclusion of a penetrating study: "The New Testament deepens our understanding of self-deception by seeing it not just as the way the human mind works nor as an

inevitability of human existence but as a cause of sin (an initiating act) and as a result of demonic evil (fate). Our understanding of self-deception is also deepened in that the condition is seen not just against oneself and others but also against God" (Dan O. Via, Jr., *Self-Deception and Wholeness in Paul and Matthew* [Minneapolis: Fortress Press, 1990], 138). The question is, Is there no self-deception on our part in this assessment of others?

18. Johnston, *Evangelicals at an Impasse*, 15–47; Coleman, *Issues of Theological Warfare*, 107–144.

19. Including the women, African-Americans, and Third World people subjugated or coopted by fundamentalist male European-Americans.

20. This interpretation of the parable of the weeds among the wheat is "legitimate." It is based upon the critical study of one of the meaning-producing dimensions of this parable in Matthew—the dimension elucidated by a structural exegesis. See Patte, *The Gospel according to Matthew*, 193–95. This view that appropriate decisions are taken by considering the positive features of a situation—while the decisions taken in terms of the negative features of a situation are always inappropriate—is also a characteristic of this meaning-producing dimension in other parts of Matthew.

21. As Michel de Certeau emphasizes in his insightful study, *Croire: une pratique de la différence*. (Urbino: Centro Internazionale di Semiotica e di Linguistica, 1981), 8–13.

22. A paraphrase of Tillich's definition of "faith" as "ultimate concern" (Paul Tillich, *The Dynamics of Faith* [New York: Harper & Row, 1957]).

23. For this definition of the basic dimension of faith, see again Tillich, *Dynamics of Faith*; and Patte, *Religious Dimensions*, 111–28.

24. Critical readings that bring to understanding ordinary readings different from ours commonly appear to us to be "artificial word games," even though they are not. Yet a critical reading not based upon an ordinary reading would be.

25. Without entering a theoretical discussion, I need to specify that I adopt the general definitions of text provided by Ricoeur, "any discourse fixed in writing" ("tout discours fixé par l'écriture") and by Greimas, "the semantic representation of a discourse" (resulting from the process of "textualization"), with the understanding, underscored in different ways by Ricoeur and Greimas, that a text has some of the characteristics of a discourse (but not all of them) and acquires other distinctive characteristics. See Paul Ricoeur, "Qu'est-ce qu'un texte? Expliquer et comprendre," in *Hermeneutik und Dialektik, Aufsätze II: Hans-Georg Gadamer zum 70. Geburtstag* (Tübingen: J.C.B. Mohr, 1970), 181–200; Eng. trans. in Paul Ricoeur, *Hermeneutics and the Human Sciences* (Cambridge: Cambridge University Press, 1981); and A. J. Greimas and J. Courtés, *Semiotics and Language: An Analytical Dictionary*, 340–42. This definition is sufficient for my present concern, which is to elucidate the "praxis" issue of the power-authority of a text.

26. When a distinction is not made between "text" and "meaningful text," one can say that each time one reads a "text," one reads a different "text" (the text as previously interpreted)—a view emphasized by Stanley Fish in *Is There a Text in This Class? The Authority of Interpretive Communities* (Cambridge: Harvard University Press, 1980). But when this distinction is made, the fact that when rereading a text someone reads it differently demonstrates that the reader (rather than the text)

has been transformed by the first reading. The text itself (the markings on the pages) has not changed. What has changed is the reader, who comes to the text with different kinds of preunderstandings—as a different person—and consequently produces with the text a different kind of meaning.

27. This view that the text has a "fixed meaning" is presupposed by any one-dimensional critical exegetical practice (each time the quest for "the" true meaning of the text), even when the practitioners are very sophisticated literary critics or advocacy scholars who profess a view of the text as "weaving" (the second metaphor). This characteristic of one-dimensional critical exegeses is typified by the arresting opening sentence of Jane Schaberg's comments on Luke (which also implicitly links meaning with power-authority—a fixed "dangerous" effect of the text upon readers): "The Gospel of Luke is an extremely dangerous text, perhaps the most dangerous in the Bible" ("Luke," in *The Women's Bible Commentary*, Carol A. Newsom and Sharon H. Ringe, eds. (Louisville, Ky.: Westminster/John Knox Press; London: SPCK, 1992), 275.

28. David Miller, "The Question of the Book: Religion as Texture," *Text and Textuality, Semeia 40* (1987) 57.

29. Miller, "The Question of the Book," 57; see also 58–62.

30. Miller, "The Question of the Book," 58–62.

31. Robert P. Scharlemann, "Theological Text," *Text and Textuality, Semeia 40* (1987) 8.

32. Hans-Georg Gadamer, *Truth and Method*, 91–119. For an excellent summary of this debate, see David Tracy, "Interpretation of the Bible and Interpretation Theory," in Robert M. Grant and David Tracy, *A Short History of the Interpretation of the Bible*, 153–66.

33. For instance, Paul Ricoeur writes: "Dialogue is an exchange of questions and answers, there is no exchange of this sort between the writer and the reader. The writer does not respond to the reader. Rather, the book divides the act of writing and the act of reading into two sides, between which there is no communication. The reader is absent from the writing; the writer is absent from the act of reading" (*Hermeneutics and the Human Sciences*, 146–47, in the essay entitled "What Is a Text?").

34. Ricoeur writes: "The distanciation in which this [Gadamer's] hermeneutics tends to see a sort of ontological fall from grace appears as a positive component of being for the text; it characteristically belongs to interpretation, not as its contrary, but as its condition. The moment of distanciation is implied by fixation in writing" (*Hermeneutics and the Human Sciences*, 91). See also in ibid., "The Hermeneutical Function of Distanciation," esp. 131–40.

35. As Gadamer says regarding classical texts. See Gadamer, *Truth and Method*, 253–58. The argument of Ricoeur mentioned above was directed against Gadamer's emphasis on the role of the text in interpretation. Note that, once again, my goal is not to resolve this theoretical debate. I merely seek to show the plausibility of both positions that we alternatively presuppose in our reading practices.

36. I allude to the rejection of critical exegeses that use other methods (embodying other preunderstandings and interests) than the one that one uses (see chapter 2).

37. Yet this "academic context" is never totally isolated from the other contexts of our lives in specific cultures, societies, and religious milieux.

38. On the heuristic character of our choice of methods, see Tolbert, *Sowing the Gospel*, 21–34. Yet she does not raise the issue of ordinary readings.

39. By contrast, we critical exegetes might have reasons to boast of our exegetical critical interpretations: They owe much to our interpretive skills (patiently acquired through rigorous training), to our ability to read a biblical text in its original language, and to our knowledge of the history of interpretation of this text.

40. For similar points regarding critical and ordinary readings in the African context, see Gerald West, *Contextual Bible Study*.

4. Androcritical Multidimensional
   Exegetical Practices:
   An Ethical Ideal and Its Dangers

The preceding chapters have led to unexpected conclusions and perceptions. Are we ethically responsible when we perform critical exegesis? In chapter 1 I had to answer no. We fail to be ethically accountable to the many people who are directly or indirectly affected by our work. In chapter 2 searching for a methodological solution to this ethical problem, I suggested that part of this ethical failure is also a lack of methodological rigor: our exegetical practices absolutize or universalize methodologies and methods that are neither absolute nor universal. One condition for ethically responsible critical practices is that they be multidimensional. In chapter 3 it became clear that in order to be ethically responsible, the critical exegetical practices of male European-American exegetes must be both multidimensional and androcritical, since from this perspective critical exegesis is the bringing to critical understanding of ordinary readings, including those other than our own.

A Reflection to Be Continued

I hope that by now these conclusions and many others that can be drawn from the preceding chapters make sense. I am aware that they may not be demonstrated to the satisfaction of many of my colleagues—biblical scholars and especially male European-American exegetes. Thus you might be tempted to put down this book, push it out of your mind, and return to your critical study of the Bible, and continue working as usual.

But even if my solutions do not convince you, I am sure you can recognize the seriousness of the problems. We cannot continue promoting apartheid, racism, sexism, oppression, and injustice in all its forms through our critical studies of the Bible. And this is what we are doing when we practice critical biblical studies as usual. We cannot remain deaf to the cries of the many victims of an oppression that we condone. Thanks to the voices of feminist, African-American, and other advocacy scholars and liberation theologians, as well as to the voices of post-Holocaust scholars, it becomes increasingly difficult to ignore these cries. And if you are still tempted by the "business as usual" routine, please consider why you perform critical biblical studies year after year and ask yourself this: Is my critical exegetical practice fulfilling my vocation? I suspect that there is a tension between your practice and your vocation. Then should you not ask yourself: Does it make sense for me to continue on the same track, even though this work is largely ineffectual?

Thus rather than rejecting my suggestions as insufficiently established or as inappropriately justified, I want to urge you to correct my points, revise my arguments, refine my remarks, and ultimately sharpen my suggestions. It is clear that my reflections are unfinished. Add to them. How should they be implemented for the study of specific texts in various contexts? In the classroom? I have made suggestions that I will now present more systematically. But they are incomplete. Complete them. Devise practices that will help us to be ethically responsible. It is only through the contributions of many that appropriate critical exegetical practices will be progressively developed and implemented. A whole series of critical exegetical practices are needed so as to interpret the Bible in an ethically responsible way in different contexts.

Of course, I am myself quite convinced of the legitimacy and the value of my own proposal. I stand by it and strive to implement it in the various situations in which I find myself. Yet my proposal also underscores that any practice that remains one-dimensional (at any level) must fail to be ethically responsible, because it has absolutized a perspective. Thus, precisely because I am convinced that my proposals are legitimate and valid, I am asking you to develop your own proposals for ethically responsible exegetical practices.

An Androcritical Multidimensional
Exegetical Practice: In Sum

In order to avoid confusion about the androcritical multidimensional exegetical practice that in my view should allow male European-American critical exegetes to be ethically responsible as they carry out their vocation, I provide here a list of its main ten features, followed by some explanations. This is a way of more systematically presenting the main points made above.

> 1. An androcritical multidimensional exegesis is a practice of critical exegesis envisioned by certain male European-American biblical scholars who seek to be accountable to those affected by their work.

Ethical accountability in exegetical practice demands that the interpreter acknowledge and affirm the context from which he or she reads the Bible. For me, this means adopting an androcritical perspective. I call "androcritical" the perspective of those male European-American biblical scholars who share a threefold experience: (1) We have been fundamentally challenged in our interpretative and pedagogical practices by feminist, womanist, mujerista, African-American, Hispanic-American, Native American, and/or third-world liberation theologians and biblical scholars (see chapter 1). (2) We strive to respond constructively to this challenge by radically transforming our practices as critical exegetes and teachers. (3) We acknowledge that all our work as critical biblical scholars is marked by the fact that we are male European-Americans. Since this kind of experience is relatively new, the androcritical movement is best described as emerging. Yet it does exist. I stumbled into it, surprised to discover that what I thought was a personal struggle is shared by so many.[1] We are dispersed throughout the world and thus are very different from one another. Thus our efforts to reconceive the critical exegetical task are quite widespread.

Androcritical exegesis is one particular androcritical effort to respond constructively to the challenge of advocacy scholars. It is "*androcritical*" also in the sense that it is critical of male European-American exegetes who do not acknowledge the contextual character of their work. Making explicit the standpoint from which I speak is an essential step in this process.

My conception of androcritical exegesis as an issue of ethical responsibility owes its specificity to my personal context. Because I, a male European-American exegete, teach in a North American context at Vanderbilt University, I am particularly challenged by feminist and African-American scholars. I remain influenced also by my European upbringing as a French Huguenot (with a childhood memory of my community's efforts to struggle against anti-Semitism during World War II) and by a two-year experience in Africa. I am a Protestant, active in and committed to the church. I am a semiotician; semiotics provides me with an interdisciplinary perspective that acknowledges its own cultural character and thus the legitimacy of a plurality of methodologies. I have pointed out, in passing, the role of these different aspects of my identity in my reflections; in the process I acknowledge my contextual and post-modern perspective.

But despite its specificity, my conception of androcritical exegesis is an effort to address concerns about the vocation shared by most male European-American critical exegetes. Far from demanding that we forsake our vocation, the androcritical exegetical practices that I envision should allow us to fulfill it more effectively (see chapter 3). Indeed, I insist (against proposals from certain of my androcritical colleagues and of advocacy scholars) that our task should remain a critical exegetical task (rather than a hermeneutical task).[2] In sum, my post-modern perspective also entails that I remain modern. This ambivalence of my androcritical proposal is not problematic: An androcritical project should include such tensions and thus ever be an unfinished business, calling for the participation of others who will be affirmed in their otherness.

> 2. The androcritical exegetical practice that I envision as a way of making our work ethically responsible needs to be multidimensional in the sense that it needs to acknowledge as equally legitimate several (rather than one) critical readings of each given text. Consequently, although it often involves the presentation of a new interpretation, its main task is the presentation of existing interpretations.

For greater clarity, it is best to refer to a concrete example: my androcritical multidimensional exegetical study, *Discipleship according to the Sermon on the Mount*. I present in it four critical exegeses of the Sermon on the Mount, each of which is heavily dependent on an interpretation (or a group of interpretations) that already exists. The contribution of this multidimensional study is to show that each is as legitimate as the others, even though they are very different and at times contradictory. This is clear as soon as I list the four interpretations I present: Strecker's;[3] Luz's;[4] Tilborg's and Patte's;[5] and an interpretation developed out of Edwards's proposals.[6]

These four existing critical exegeses are not merely reproduced. I propose a critical interpretation of each of them (including my own) from a specific and unified perspective—an androcritical perspective. This multidimensional exegesis is androcritical, among other reasons, because it critically examines existing interpretations by male European-American exegetes. Rather than being a study of the biblical text itself, an androcritical multidimensional exegesis is a critical examination of existing interpretations.[7] As discussed below in theses 4 and 5, these interpretations do not need to be critical studies; they can be ordinary readings and literary uses of the Bible. Yet in the present situation, it is important to begin with an androcritical multidimensional review of existing critical exegeses.

> 3. This androcritical multidimensional exegesis and traditional criti-
> cal reviews of the scholarship are based on diametrically opposed pre-
> suppositions about critical exegesis.

From the foregoing, one could conclude that an androcritical multidimensional exegesis is nothing more than a kind of critical review of
the scholarship, such as Stanton's "The Origin and Purpose of
Matthew's Gospel: Matthean Scholarship from 1945 to 1980."[8] Yet this
is far from true.

Note the presuppositions upon which a traditional critical review is
based. Stanton presents the diverse critical interpretations of the
Gospel according to Matthew in order to elucidate the "advances in
our [scholarly] understanding of this gospel,"[9] that is, those points that
can be considered as established, because alternative interpretations of
them have been soundly refuted; and the issues about which "questions
must be pressed,"[10] because they have not yet been satisfactorily resolved by Matthean scholarship. The four fundamental presuppositions here are that the diverse critical exegeses represent a collective
scholarly effort (1) to interpret the text of the Gospel according to
Matthew in its historical and cultural context, with (2) the goal of progressively establishing "the" critical understanding of this Gospel, that
is, its single legitimate meaning. Moreover, (3) the several and very diverse critical methods complement each other by contributing to the
establishment of *the* critical understanding of the text, a new method
advancing *the* understanding of the Gospel according to Matthew by
allowing scholars to clarify certain points, without which this Gospel
could not be properly understood. (4) It is further presupposed that
this critical interpretation, once established, provides the basis for dismissing or correcting unwarranted precritical interpretations and their
assumptions or preunderstandings.

These presuppositions are plausible as long as one exclusively focuses on the outcome of the process of interpretation. But the opposite
presuppositions are at least as plausible when one focuses on the
process of interpretation itself:

1. Is a critical exegesis the interpretation of the text in and of itself?
Or, is it not as plausible to acknowledge that a critical exegesis is always
the interpretation of existing interpretations of the text?[11]

2. Should the goal of critical exegesis be envisioned as the establishment of *the* critical understanding of the text, its single legitimate
meaning? Or, is it not as plausible to acknowledge that any text is polysemic,[12] and thus that it offers a plurality of potential legitimate meanings,[13] and that a goal of critical exegesis is the elucidation of a plurality
of equally critical understandings of the text?[14]

3. Should the several critical methods be viewed as complementing each other, despite their diversity? Or, is it not as plausible to view them as providing the means to establish the legitimacy of different potential meanings of the text? Would this not better account for the very diverse exegetical conclusions reached by the uses of these various methods?[15]

4. Should the relation between critical exegesis and precritical interpretations (ordinary readings) be envisioned as one-directional and antagonistic (exegesis seeking to overcome mistaken precritical interpretations)? Or, is it not as plausible to envision this relationship as interactive and constructive? For instance, are not our critical exegeses preceded by and rooted in "hunches" that we verify by our critical investigations? Are not such hunches precritical interpretations? Then, could one not envision one of the main tasks of critical exegesis as the bringing to critical understanding of precritical interpretations?[16]

As is clear by now, the androcritical multidimensional exegesis I propose adopts these alternative presuppositions. With such presuppositions, one has quite a different attitude toward the diversity of existing critical exegeses. Until it is proven otherwise, one can suspect that these critical exegeses are basically legitimate, even if they are incompatible with one another—while traditional critical reviews presuppose that they are to be suspected of being illegitimate until proven otherwise.

I have attempted to show that each of these presuppositions is at least as plausible as the corresponding opposite presupposition traditionally held in biblical scholarship. Yet it might be useful to clarify them further by looking at them from the perspective of the traditional practices of critical exegesis.

> 4. The proposed androcritical multidimensional exegesis presupposes that any critical exegesis is the interpretation of existing interpretations, rather than a direct interpretation of the text.

This presupposition does not deny that a given critical exegesis provides new insights about the text itself. Rather, it underscores the process through which these insights are gained: through the interpretation of one or several existing interpretations.

Exegetes for whom biblical scholarship is a collective effort would agree that in many instances a critical exegesis is primarily the interpretation of one or several existing critical interpretations of a text, rather than a direct interpretation of the text itself. In such cases, we read the critical interpretations first; then we study the text to verify the extent to which these interpretations are or are not supported by the textual evidence and to learn something new about the text. A critical review is an extreme form of this type of critical exegesis.[17]

Yet I want to go further and claim that *any* critical exegesis is the interpretation of existing interpretations. This is true even when the critical exegesis presents itself as the interpretation of the text itself (for instance, through the rigorous use of a new critical method).[18] Once again, I do not deny that such an exegesis provides new critical insights about the text itself. What I want to underscore is that (1) the fresh critical examination of the text owes its originality to the fact that one looks at the text from a different perspective, with new questions and assumptions in mind;[19] and (2) this new perspective and these new questions and assumptions originate in existing interpretations, including "preunderstandings" of the text, which are nothing else than preinterpretations (possibly barely developed and crude) of the text or, better, *precritical interpretations of the text*.[20]

Consequently, for this androcritical multidimensional exegesis, any given critical exegesis is either (1) a second-level interpretation (a critical interpretation of existing precritical interpretations) or (2) a third-level interpretation (a critical interpretation of existing critical exegeses, each of which is itself a critical interpretation of existing precritical interpretations); or again, and most often, (3) a combination of second- and third-level interpretations (the critical interpretation of existing precritical interpretations plays a direct role even in a third-level interpretation).

> 5. This androcritical multidimensional exegesis presupposes that a critical exegesis bring to critical understanding a precritical interpretation, or ordinary reading.

The plausibility of this presupposition appears when one notes that in most instances, the practice of critical exegesis has a polemical edge that at least implies a precritical interpretation. Critical biblical scholarship has always been practiced in order to marshal the evidence that allows one to reject certain kinds of interpretations as uncritical, such as dogmatic interpretations of the church (e.g., in nineteenth-century biblical scholarship) or other "inappropriate" (e.g., fundamentalist, integrist) interpretations. My point is simply that before beginning a critical exegesis, exegetes feel in a precritical way that an interpretation is inadequate, misleading, or even erroneous, and thus feel that an alternate interpretation that they at least dimly envision is appropriate and true. It is this felt interpretation (with its polemical and constructive components) that I call a precritical interpretation. This precritical interpretation plays an essential and primary role in the process of critical interpretation. Even though it might end up being significantly refined and complemented, it motivates the exegete to proceed to a critical exegesis (which would be purposeless without it). This implies that no critical exegesis is a disinterested interpretation of the biblical text, a point to which I shall return. This underscores once again, but in a different way, why in my view it is plausible to say that a critical exegesis brings to critical understanding an ordinary reading (a precritical interpretation).

> 6. The androcritical multidimensional exegesis proposed in this book envisions the task of critical exegesis as a theological task, a form of contextual theology.

This statement regarding the nature of the task of critical exegesis derives from the recognition that a critical exegesis aims at bringing to critical understanding a precritical interpretation that belongs to the realm of faith, the realm of convictions felt as self-evidently true.[21] Even though the ordinary readings that are brought to critical understanding by exegeses are often against traditional faith-interpretations by churches and religious groups, they nevertheless are the expression of convictions that belong to a faith (defined as a system of convictions), possibly a liberal or even a secular faith. Saying that these interpretations are precritical is the same as saying that they are convictional and thus belong to the realm of faith.

This observation is far from being some gratuitous quibble about vocabulary. It allows us to recover a clearer sense of the task and vocation that we pursue in our practice as male European-American exegetes. By recognizing that critical exegesis aims at bringing to critical understanding an existing faith-interpretation (a precritical interpretation), we actually acknowledge that the critical exegetical task is a theological task, according to its classic definition by Anselm:[22] *fides quaerens intellectum*, "faith seeking understanding."

The implications of this acknowledgment are many. Here, it is enough to note two. First, acknowledging the theological character of our critical task allows us to consider our own precritical interpretations and those of other people in a positive light. As faith-interpretations they have an intrinsic legitimacy (as the *sensus fidei*, or "spontaneous faith" of the people),[23] even though they need to be refined by being understood and even though their validity needs to be critically assessed. In other words, each of these precritical interpretations can be viewed as the perception of something true (legitimate) about the biblical text, even though the expression of this truth might be inappropriate (invalid).

Second, this acknowledgment allows us to recognize that each of these precritical interpretations is *contextual* in nature; they are faith-interpretations that are directly related to faith-questions, each arising out of a specific context. Just as there are necessarily different theologies because they are contextual in nature—a point underscored by liberation theologians[24]—so are there necessarily different critical exegeses of a given text, because they also are contextual through the precritical interpretations they bring to critical understanding.

> 7. An androcritical multidimensional exegesis is a critical exegesis practiced by male European-Americans who acknowledge that their exegetical practices are contextual theological practices arising out of the specific contexts of male European-American exegetes.

As soon as one acknowledges that any critical exegesis is contextual, one has to expect a plurality of different but equally legitimate critical interpretations of the same text. This is, of course, the present reality, in which we find, alongside traditional critical exegeses, a growing number of critical interpretations of the Bible that make their contextual character explicit—those of feminist,[25] womanist,[26] and African-American[27] biblical scholars (soon to be joined by mujerista, Hispanic-American, and other advocacy critics). Traditional critical exegeses are no less contextual, even though in most instances they fail to acknowledge and may even conceal their contextuality. They address the interests and concerns of male European-American exegetes by providing critical understandings of their precritical interpretations. This is what an androcritical exegesis acknowledges and seeks to make explicit in its practices, taking note that the plurality of male European-American critical exegeses arises out of a plurality of distinct contexts in which white male exegetes have specific interests and concerns. Consequently, the androcritical exegetical project is not to replace our disinterested practices by interested ones. All critical exegeses are interested, whether or not we are aware of it. It is therefore a matter of elucidating the interested character of our previous exegeses and making explicit this character in our new exegeses. As we self-consciously do so, we will be led to evaluate our choices of interests and concerns (Are they the most urgent ones? Are they in conflict with other people's interests?) and our choice of practices (Is it the most effective way to address these interests and concerns?).

This androcritical exegesis can be, and needs to be, practiced from the outside. This is what other advocacy exegetes do when they expose the androcentrism and Eurocentrism of male European-American exegeses and eventually denounce their patriarchalism and/or racism.

Their contributions to the development of androcritical exegesis are essential. Without them, we would not even be able to envision androcritical exegesis. Yet beyond this overall critique of male European-American exegetical practices, we also need to conceive androcritical exegesis from the inside as a multidimensional practice in the same way that feminists progressively discovered that they must envision a plurality of feminisms and thus of feminist interpretations.

My main point is that male European-American exegetes should themselves practice androcritical exegesis. We must become self-conscious about the interested character of our critical exegeses. That is, we must become aware that they are shaped by our specific interests and concerns as male European-Americans in given historical contexts. We must do this for the sake of others. For as long as our exegeses are not multidimensional and androcritical, they are not ethically responsible. Instead, they contribute to the oppression of the oppressed by demanding of them that they forsake their identities, values, and valid concerns (see chapter 1).

But it is not solely or primarily for the sake of others that we should practice multidimensional androcritical exegeses. Actually *we shall truly be engaged in such a project only if we clearly perceive that it is in our own interest to do so.* The ethical problem that we have to overcome is not merely the one that consists of the exclusion and suppression of the interpretations of the Bible by women, African-Americans, and other oppressed groups. We also have very effectively suppressed our own readings, denying any ownership and interest in them. Through our critical interpretations of the Bible we forsake our own identities, values, and valid concerns. Then we wonder why our critical work engenders "the strange silence of the Bible in the Church."[28] Oh yes! We male European-Americans urgently need to practice multidimensional androcritical exegeses *for our own sake.*

> 8. Androcritical multidimensional exegesis as I envision it presupposes that the plurality of critical exegeses establishes a plurality of equally critical and legitimate, though different, understandings of a given text because each critical exegesis elucidates one of the several meaning-producing dimensions of the text, specifically, the one that gave rise to the precritical interpretation.

The plausibility of this thesis, which includes conceiving of any given text as polysemic and thus as offering to readers several potential semantic coherences, appears most clearly as we (1) consider the critical interpretations that result from the use of different critical methods and as we (2) note that each interpretation underscores certain features of the text. Each points to a certain meaning-producing dimension of the text as the primary evidence for its distinct conclusion regarding the coherent view of the meaning of the text. When this is acknowledged, the contextual character of each of the critical exegeses appears; one can perceive how each addresses the specific concerns and interests of one or another group of male European-Americans—or of a group dominated by us. This puts us in a position to become andro-critical in another way; by assessing the ethical validity of choosing one or the other of these critically established meanings of the text (e.g., diverse views of discipleship).

Most of the existing critical exegeses by male European-American exegetes were originally done with the presupposition that there were two tasks to do: (1) to establish *the* (single and universally true) meaning of the text, and consequently (2) to disprove all other interpretations. Thus when two critical studies reached different conclusions, a critical debate ensued. Consider, for instance, the debate between Georg Strecker and Ulrich Luz. Does Matthew's teaching about the discipleship owe its coherence (i.e., its single meaning) to the historicizing of the disciples as personages belonging to a unique and unrepeatable past, the time of Jesus' ministry (Strecker)?[29] Or to a presentation of the disciples as figures of discipleship that provide the church with a vision of eschatological life toward which the church is called to orient itself (Luz)?[30] Each scholar (and his followers) is convinced that he is right and that the other is wrong, on the grounds that two incompatible interpretations cannot both be right.

But since both cases are made on the basis of strong evidence from the text, why not acknowledge that they refer to two different, coherent, meaning-producing dimensions of Matthew's presentation of the disciples? Are not these two interpretations similar to the interpretations of the black and white gestalt picture used in psychological tests, in which one perceives the faces of two persons looking at each other when focusing upon the black features, but a goblet when focusing upon the white features? From this perspective, the insistence that Matthew's presentation of the disciples has a single semantic coherence requires ignoring and denying the existence of textual evidence that presents the other coherence. Furthermore, this insistence leads one to become inconsistent in one's choice of evidence; Strecker adopts some of Luz's points that he cannot refute, even though they are in tension with his own interpretation, and vice versa.

A close examination of the debate between Strecker and Luz led me to recognize that their respective studies focus on two different, coherent, meaning-producing dimensions of the Gospel according to Matthew. As soon as one can envision the existence of two semantic coherences in a given text, one is led to recognize that other such coherences might also be expressed by the same text. Consequently, other interpretations might themselves be the elucidations of other specific, coherent, meaning-producing dimensions of the text, even if each of them claims to elucidate *the* single meaning of the text.

> 9. The practice of this androcritical multidimensional exegesis means acknowledging and affirming the legitimacy of readings that reflect the interests and concerns of groups other than male European-American groups.

The recognition of the legitimacy of several male European-American readings developed on the basis of different meaning-producing dimensions of a text is an invitation to recognize and affirm the legitimacy of other readings. The legitimacy of these other interpretations might already be established, as in the cases of interpretations by feminist, African-American, and other advocacy scholars. In other cases, such as the interpretations of ordinary readers (including students and lay members of the churches in various social, cultural, and religious contexts), the legitimacy of these interpretations might still need to be elucidated. As teachers/facilitators, our role might be to empower these ordinary readers to bring to critical understanding (and thus refine) their own readings. In this way we put our interpretive skills and knowledge at the service of these ordinary readers. This is our contribution to them.

Conversely, these ordinary readers give us their distinctive interpretations, which are necessary contributions to the ongoing process of bringing to critical understanding our own interpretations. In order to acknowledge and affirm the interpretations, we need to understand their distinctiveness. Comparisons with legitimate interpretations that differ from ours best elucidate the distinctiveness of our conclusions regarding the teaching and the meaning-producing dimension of the text that particularly concerns or interests us. This face-to-face dialogue with other interpreters whose otherness I respect is a necessary step in recognizing and affirming as mine the specificity of my interpretation. In sum, acknowledging the legitimacy of other readers' interpretations is a necessary part of my critical exegetical endeavor; without it, I could not acknowledge and affirm the distinctiveness of my own interpretation.

> 10. Finally, the practice of this androcritical multidimensional exegesis necessarily confronts us with a moral choice when we ask each of the various legitimate interpretations the following questions: What

is its relative value? Is it helpful? Is it harmful? Who benefits? Who is hurt? We have to assume responsibility for our choice of one reading as the most significant for us.

As we acknowledge and affirm the legitimacy of a plurality of interpretations in addition to our own, we discover that reading a text always involves selecting an interpretation because consciously or not we feel it is particularly significant for us. This is true in the case of one-dimensional exegeses, even though in this case one overlooks that a value judgment took place. This is also true in the case of androcritical multidimensional exegeses; whether we like it or not, we end up valuing one reading as more significant than the others. But in this case, we are in a position to assume responsibility for our choice. This is a question of validity and should not be confused with a question of legitimacy. This value judgment involves raising issues similar to those raised in chapter 1. This step is necessary in our effort to be ethically responsible as critical exegetes, although we run the danger of being caught in the web of a hierarchical structure (as I noted in this book's introduction). But an androcritical multidimensional practice should, to some extent, alleviate this danger because it demands from us to make a value judgment not only in terms of our own interests and concerns, but also in terms of those of other people. Nevertheless, this value judgment is fraught with ambivalence; it could easily lead us once again to speak for others, patronizing them, or to listen to them, coopting them. Thus the value judgment through which we assume responsibility for our choice of reading must be practiced by speaking *with* others (as discussed on pp. 23–25), and thus it calls for a return to the acknowledgment and affirmation of the legitimacy of other people's readings.

These last comments once again appear to betray our vocation as critical biblical scholars. Is it our role to choose among readings on the basis of a value judgment? A few concluding comments seek to clarify this point by showing how an androcritical multidimensional practice fulfills our value-laden vocation as critical exegetes.

A Call to a Self-Conscious Practice of Our Vocation

In sum, my proposal is that in order to be ethically accountable, male European-American exegetes must *practice* critical exegesis in a multidimensional and *androcritical* way. In addition, in order to be ethically responsible, we must assume responsibility for our choice of one reading as the one that is most significant for us. By underscoring the terms "practice" and "androcritical," I seek to signal both continuity and discontinuity with what we are commonly doing in our task as critical exegetes. By keeping accountability and responsibility in tension, I seek to signal the ambivalence of our task. I emphasize that this proposal concerns the practice of critical exegesis to make clear that it does not demand that we abandon either the critical methods we use or the ultimate goals that we pursue through our exegetical research and teaching, ultimate goals that define our vocation as critical exegetes (see chapter 3). Furthermore, it does *not* demand that we reject the history of scholarship and our own previous critical interpretations. On the contrary, a multidimensional exegesis involves affirming the basic legitimacy of the diversity of existing critical interpretations, and thus demands a *positive* appropriation of the history of scholarship in all its richness.

This proposal is a matter of practice in the sense that it concerns the ways we male European-American exegetes use critical methods, the ways we consider the results of our critical exegeses, the ways we conceive their interrelations with other interpretations, and the ways we present our interpretations in our teaching and publications. I want to argue that the need for a different critical exegetical practice appears when we acknowledge our fundamental reasons for using these critical methods and for pursuing our vocation as critical exegetes (something that we rarely do). As a result of this rare acknowledgment, we discover that our current practices are at odds with these reasons. Our practical uses of critical methods and their results hinder or even preclude the fulfillment of our vocation, even though these methods were developed as a means for fulfilling it. Thus, this is a call to self-consciously reclaim our sense of vocation as critical exegetes and to make sure that our critical practices truly help us fulfill this vocation.

By calling our exegetical practice androcritical, I acknowledge that we male European-American exegetes have a different sense of vocation as compared with that of feminist, African-American, and other advocacy biblical scholars. In their critical biblical studies, they adopt an advocacy stance on behalf of one or another specific group, while in our critical studies we do not adopt such a stance on behalf of these specific groups.[31] We have a different sense of vocation. As we become self-conscious of it, we discover that both our vocation and our exegetical practices are governed by interests and concerns that are those of males and of European-Americans in specific contexts. Despite our denials, we also have an advocacy stance. It is on behalf of male European-Americans (usually, a subgroup of them) that we practice critical exegeses. Being androcritical involves acknowledging this fact.

Adopting an androcritical stance, radical as this might seem, does *not* demand that we abandon our specific vocation. As we become self-conscious of our vocation, we have to acknowledge that our present ex-egetical practices are androcentric, as feminists insist,[32] and Eurocen-tric, as African-American exegetes[33] emphasize. Furthermore, we are led to recognize that androcentrism and Eurocentrism are the sources of our lack of accountability in our critical exegetical practices. But as we saw, the solution to this ethical problem is *not* a rejection of our maleness and our Europeanness. Rather, we are called to acknowledge and self-consciously claim what we have been doing all along: pursuing our vocation as critical exegetes in order to address certain concerns and interests of European-American males.

In most instances, these concerns and interests are, in themselves, quite appropriate and valid; we can proudly affirm them as our own. But by acknowledging them, we transform our ways of using critical methods, appraising our own interpretations, and presenting them. We become critical of our andro*centrism* and Euro*centrism* in the sense that we reject these absolutizations (but not our maleness and our Euro-peanness as such). In sum, our practice of critical exegesis becomes androcritical. As a result, ethical accountability becomes an actual possibility.

When our critical practices are both androcritical and multidimen-sional, ethical accountability in critical exegesis becomes even more a possibility, because our practices are then turned toward others and dedicated to affirming their otherness. Such practices should be "de-centered."

For instance, a pedagogical androcritical multidimensional practice would have as its goal teaching students how to bring to critical un-derstanding their own ordinary readings (*pro me* interpretations; faith-interpretations) of biblical texts. For this purpose, a plurality of critical interpretations of each given text would be presented to the students so as to make clear in each case (1) the ordinary reading or *pro me* inter-pretation that this critical study brings to critical understanding (some-thing that traditional critical exegeses usually express and hide in their conclusions); and (2) how and through what method this ordinary reading was brought to critical understanding (this involves elucidating the meaning-producing dimension of the text that the reading is fo-cused upon). By comparing their *pro me* interpretations to those of the critical studies presented in an androcritical and multidimensional way, students can recognize the specific critical reading that can serve as a model for bringing to critical understanding their own ordinary read-ing, and thus for refining it and complementing it, without abandon-ing it. In sum, they are empowered to acknowledge and affirm the legitimacy of their own contextual readings, whatever they might be.

Such a pedagogical practice of critical exegesis is not alienating; it is no longer promoting apartheid by suppressing unwanted voices. On the contrary, it should promote the affirmation of the otherness of others and of their interpretations, and thus be ever mindful of the other and her or his need. It should promote justice.

Back to the Beginning and Its Ambivalence

The question with which I want to conclude is: Will such an andro-critical multidimensional practice of critical exegesis truly promote justice? Theoretically, it should. But will it? We cannot verify it as long as our concern is exclusively for accountability through an androcritical, multidimensional perspective. In this case, our role is to identify and affirm what is legitimate and good in an interpretation (the wheat), an attitude that is incompatible with negative judgment and condemnation of what is bad (the weeds). On the basis of the assessment of the legitimacy of various readings, we cannot demand that others change their ways, and we cannot even evaluate the validity of our own interpretations. For this evaluation, we have to ask another set of questions and make a value judgment regarding the relative value of diverse interpretations.

Going back to chapter 1, we have to ask: Are we ethically responsible when we perform this critical (androcritical multidimensional) interpretation? When we adopt as our own this or that interpretation? These are the questions through which we assume ethical responsibility for the effect of our interpretations upon others. (See above, thesis 10.) These are important questions that set up clear criteria and norms with the help of one or another ethical theory; essential questions that allow us to declare one interpretation valid and another one invalid; necessary questions that call us to repentance. We have been called to repentance by discovering that our traditional critical practices betrayed many people and failed to be accountable for and contributed to the oppression of those who are directly or indirectly affected by our work. We cannot help but raise these questions—and go back to chapter 1.

But we must do so with caution. We have to be ready to abandon these questions of responsibility as soon as we raise them, so that we may quickly turn again to the androcritical multidimensional acknowledgment and affirmation of the legitimacy of various readings. Let us remember that the questions of responsibility are dangerous; they put us in a position of hierarchical superiority over all other readers and thus have the potential of making us oppressors. Therefore, our practices need to maintain the very tensions that this book represents. Striving toward the ideal—through androcritical multidimensional practices, by affirming the legitimacy of various readings—should keep us ethically accountable. But verifying the value of these practices—by using the question of responsibility, which pragmatically expects that we cannot help but stumble if not fall—should keep us in check.

Maintaining these tensions and this ambivalence is not that difficult. As we focus on the ideal and seek to implement androcritical, multidimensional practices appropriate for our situations, we cannot help but consider pragmatic issues. We have to decide which one of the several legitimate readings is most helpful in a situation. Thus we have to identify "the problem" (see chapter 1) that we must address through our reading of the Bible.

NOTES

1. The androcritical biblical scholars' movement is related to the "men's movement" and more specifically to its trends that conceive it as parallel to and not antagonistic with feminism, as in Sam Keen, *Fire in the Belly: On Being a Man* (New York: Bantam Books, 1991). Yet an important difference is that in my understanding, androcritical biblical scholars do not mimic the feminist liberation approach, as Keen does, by claiming ourselves as victims of oppression. Rather we acknowledge that our current practices are oppressive and thus must be criticized in this light.

2. I refer, for instance, to the group of biblical scholars gathered around Bernard Lategan of Stellenbosch University, South Africa, in the Center for Contextual Hermeneutics. Although I believe their emphasis on hermeneutics is inappropriate for transforming the teaching of biblical studies in the classroom in South Africa, it is most appropriate for the other aspects of the amazing work they do in the struggle against apartheid in all its forms. In brief, in a theory of reading as the production of meaning, which is appropriately called "hermeneutics," there is room for the role of the text in this production of meaning, and thus for exegesis as the description of this role in the production of meaning. See J. Severino Croatto, *Biblical Hermeneutics: Toward a Theory of Reading as the Production of Meaning* (Maryknoll, N.Y.: Orbis Books, 1987), from which I borrowed the categories used in the preceding comments.

3. Georg Strecker, *The Sermon on the Mount: An Exegetical Commentary* (Nashville: Abingdon Press, 1988); and to a lesser extent idem, *Der Weg der Gerechtigkeit: Untersuchung zur Theologie des Matthäus* (Göttingen: Vandenhoeck and Ruprecht, 1962). This interpretation also presents the work of a few other scholars who happen to have a similar interpretation, such as Jack D. Kingsbury, "The Verb *Akolouthein* ('to Follow') as an Index of Matthew's View of His Community," *Journal of Biblical Literature* 97 (1978); idem, *Matthew as Story* (Philadelphia: Fortress Press, 1986); and Jean Zumstein, *La condition du croyant dans l'Evangile selon Matthieu* (Göttingen: Vandenhoeck and Ruprecht, 1977).

4. Ulrich Luz, *Matthew 1–7: A Commentary* (Minneapolis: Augsburg, 1989); and idem, "The Disciples in the Gospel according to Matthew," *The Interpretation of Matthew*, Graham Stanton, ed. (Philadelphia: Fortress Press; London: SPCK, 1983), 98–128. This interpretation also takes into account W. D. Davies and D. C.

Allison, Jr., *A Critical and Exegetical Commentary on the Gospel According to Saint Matthew*; and W. D. Davies, *The Setting of the Sermon on the Mount*.

5. Sjef van Tilborg, *The Sermon on the Mount as an Ideological Intervention: A Reconstruction of Meaning* (Assen/Maastricht: Van Gorcum, 1986); and D. Patte, *The Gospel according to Matthew: A Structural Commentary on Matthew's Faith*.

6. Richard A. Edwards, *Matthew's Story of Jesus* (Philadelphia: Fortress Press, 1985); and idem, "Uncertain Faith: Matthew's Portrait of the Disciples," in *Discipleship in the New Testament*, F. F. Segovia, ed. (Philadelphia: Fortress Press, 1985). Since he does not present a detailed study of the Sermon, in this case I had to develop it myself.

7. I shall argue below that this is what any critical exegesis does, even when it pretends to be a study of the text by itself. An androcritical exegesis simply makes it explicit.

8. Stanton, "The Origin and Purpose of Matthew's Gospel," in *Aufstieg und Niedergang der Römischen Welt* II.25.3., (Berlin: Walter de Gruyter, 1983), pp. 1879–1951, a very helpful review essay.

9. Stanton, "The Origin and Purpose of Matthew's Gospel," 1944; see also 1895, passim.

10. Stanton, "The Origin and Purpose of Matthew's Gospel," 1938; cf. 1899, passim. In one way or another, throughout his essay, Stanton underscores "the weaknesses of current . . . critical work on Matthew" (p. 1899).

11. If not, why are we always referring to other interpretations?

12. One can at the very least recognize that certain texts are polysemic. Such are the parables, as recent studies have emphasized: see, John Dominic Crossan, *Cliffs of Fall: Paradox and Polyvalence in the Parables of Jesus* (New York: Seabury Press, 1980); and Bernard Brandon Scott, *Hear Then the Parable: A Commentary on the Parables of Jesus* (Philadelphia: Fortress Press, 1989), where multiple readings of the parables are provided. Texts involving irony are also clearly polysemic. See, for instance, on 1 Corinthians 1–4, Karl A. Plank, *Paul and the Irony of Affliction*, Semeia Studies (Atlanta: Scholars Press, 1987). Next, the polysemy of any figurative text should be recognized since a figure (e.g., a metaphor) involves a double semantic investment. It is then, difficult to imagine any biblical text which would not be at least somewhat polysemic. From the perspective of semiotic theory, any text as semantic representation of a discourse is necessarily polysemic.

13. As was emphasized by Mary Ann Tolbert, *Perspectives on the Parables: An Approach to Multiple Interpretations* (Philadelphia: Fortress Press, 1979).

14. Of course, this does not mean that each time one should be expected to give equal weight to the several interpretations. One can make clear that for practical reasons, one focuses upon a given interpretation while acknowledging the legitimacy of other existing interpretations that are simply presented in summary form. A good example is provided by Timothy B. Cargal, *Restoring the Diaspora: Discursive Structure and Purpose in the Epistle of James*, SBL Dissertation Series 144 (Atlanta: Scholars Press, 1993).

15. This point can be illustrated by considering the following recent studies on the Gospel of Mark (chosen for their methodological diversity, without attempting to be comprehensive): Willi Marxsen, *Mark the Evangelist: Studies on the Redaction History of the Gospel* (Nashville: Abingdon Press, 1969); Benoit Standaert, *L'Evangile de Marc: Composition et Genre Littéraire* (Brugge: Zevenkerken 1978);

Joanna Dewey, *Markan Public Debate: Literary Technique, Concentric Structure, and Theology in Mk 2:1—3:6*, SBL Dissertation Series 48 (Missoula, Mont.: Scholars Press, 1979); Vernon K. Robbins, *Jesus the Teacher: A Socio-Rhetorical Interpretation of Mark* (Philadelphia: Fortress Press, 1984); Kelber, *The Oral and the Written Gospel*; Elizabeth Struthers Malbon, *Narrative Space and Mythic Meaning in Mark* (San Francisco: Harper & Row, 1986); Ched Myers, *Binding the Strong Man: A Political Reading of Mark's Story of Jesus* (Maryknoll, N.Y.: Orbis Books, 1988); Mary Ann Tolbert, *Sowing the Gospel: Mark's World in Literary-Historical Perspective*; Robert Fowler, *Let the Reader Understand: Reader-Response Criticism and the Gospel of Mark* (Minneapolis: Fortress Press, 1991); and the essays in Janice Capel Anderson and Stephen D. Moore, *Mark and Method: New Approaches in Biblical Studies* (Minneapolis: Fortress Press, 1992). Shouldn't one acknowledge that these studies, with their different foci that reflect a diversity of critical methods, are establishing the legitimacy of different potential meanings of the text?

16. As is clarified below, these precritical interpretations are thus presupposed to be basically legitimate (rather than basically illegitimate) and include ordinary readings of all kinds that truly express how certain readers have been affected by the text. Among such authentic ordinary readings I include the uses of the Bible in literature. When they propose an unexpected reading, they reflect a meaning-producing dimension of the text that had been forgotten; they remember the text (or something about the text). Thus, their responsible interpretation is not typological ([hermeneutic] fulfillment, which exhausts the text; then the text can be discarded); as a "remembering," it is an affirmation of the text and its polysemy. See Regina M. Schwartz, "Joseph's Bones and the Resurrection of the Text: Remembering in the Bible," in *The Book and the Text: The Bible and Literary Theory* (Oxford and Cambridge, Mass.: Basil Blackwell Publisher, 1990), 40–59.

17. This is speaking about fair reviews. If, by contrast, bad reviewers merely assess the new work on the basis of previous interpretations (especially their own) held to be normative, then the reviewer has decided in advance that the work under consideration has nothing new to contribute regarding our understanding of the text.

18. For instance, when G. Bornkamm introduced the systematic use of redaction criticism in his 1948 essay, "The Stilling of the Storm in Matthew," published in English in G. Bornkamm, G. Barth, and H. J. Held, *Tradition and Interpretation in Matthew* (Philadelphia: Westminster Press, 1963).

19. This point should not surprise traditional biblical scholars. For instance, Stanton ("The Origin and Purpose of Matthew's Gospel," passim) constantly refers to the kinds "questions" and of "assumptions" that govern the work of Matthean scholars.

20. That new questions that reflect contemporary existing interpretations (or at least, contemporary issues and concerns) are raised in recent critical interpretations readily appears, for instance, in the study of Paul's Christology, even though it involves a detailed and rigorous study of its primary texts (1 and 2 Corinthians); see David Odell-Scott, *A Post-Patriarchal Christology*, American Academy of Religion Series (Atlanta: Scholars Press, 1992).

21. On this definition of faith as a system of convictions, see D. Patte, *Paul's Faith and the Power of the Gospel*, 7–27; idem, *The Gospel according to Matthew*, 4–8; and idem, *Religious Dimensions*, 103–215.

22. *St. Anselm's Proslogion*, M. J. Charlesworth, trans. (Notre Dame and London: University of Notre Dame Press, 1979).

23. On the importance of the *sensus fidei* of the people as the basis of theology according to Anselm's definition, see Albert Nolan and Richard Broderick, *To Nourish Our Faith: Theology of Liberation for South Africa* (Hilton, South Africa: Cornerstone Books, 1987), 10–29. See also Albert Nolan, *Jesus before Christianity* (Cape Town, South Africa: David Philip Publisher, 1976, 1986); and idem, *God in South Africa: The Challenge of the Gospel* (Cape Town, South Africa: David Philip Publisher; Grand Rapids: Wm. B. Eerdmans Publishing Co., 1988).

24. Such as the theologians at the Institute for Contextual Theology in Johannesburg (led by Albert Nolan), out of which came *The Kairos Document* (1986) and other similar documents, such as, more recently, *Violence, The New Kairos: Challenge to the Churches* (1990).

25. For a bibliography and samples of feminist critical interpretations, see Phyllis Trible, *God and the Rhetoric of Sexuality* (Philadelphia: Fortress Press, 1978); Elisabeth Schüssler Fiorenza, *In Memory of Her* (1983); Mary Ann Tolbert, ed., *The Bible and Feminist Hermeneutics, Semeia 28* (Atlanta: Scholars Press, 1983); Adela Yarbro Collins, ed., *Feminist Perspectives on Biblical Scholarship* (Atlanta: Scholars Press, 1985); Letty M. Russell, ed., *Feminist Interpretation of the Bible* (Philadelphia: Westminster Press, 1985); J. Cheryl Exum and Johanna W. H. Bos, eds., *Reasoning with the Foxes: Female Wit in a World of Male Power, Semeia 42* (Atlanta: Scholars Press, 1988); Peggy L. Day, ed., *Gender and Difference in Ancient Israel* (Minneapolis: Fortress Press, 1989); Carol A. Newsom and Sharon H. Ringe, eds., *The Women's Bible Commentary* (Louisville, Ky.: Westminster/John Knox Press, 1992); Claudia V. Camp and Carole R. Fontaine, eds., *Women, War and Metaphor, Semeia 61* (Atlanta: Scholars Press, 1993).

26. For instance, Renita J. Weems, *Just a Sister Away: A Womanist Vision of Women's Relationships in the Bible* (San Diego, Calif.: LuraMedia, 1988); idem, *Marriage, Sex, and Violence: Hebrew Rhetoric and Audience* (Minneapolis: Fortress Press, 1992); idem, "Reading *Her Way* through the Struggle: African American Women and the Bible," in Felder, *Stony the Road We Trod*, 57–77; and Clarice Martin, "The Haustafeln (Household Codes) in African American Biblical Interpretation: 'Free Slaves' and 'Subordinate Women,'" in Felder, Stony the Road We Trod, 206–31.

27. See e.g., Cain H. Felder, *Troubling Biblical Waters: Race, Class, and Family* (Maryknoll, N.Y.: Orbis Books, 1989), and Felder, *Stony the Road We Trod*.

28. See James Smart, *The Strange Silence of the Bible in the Church*.

29. Georg Strecker, *Der Weg der Gerechtigkeit*; and idem, "The Concept of History in Matthew," in G. Stanton, ed., *The Interpretation of Matthew* (Philadelphia: Fortress Press; London: SPCK, 1983), 67–84.

30. Ulrich Luz, "The Disciples in the Gospel according to Matthew," in Stanton, *Matthew*, 98–128; and idem, *Matthew 1–7: A Commentary*. The figurative character of Luz's interpretation appears most clearly in its treatment of the Sermon.

31. Even if we try, we can never do so to the satisfaction of these groups since their interests are not fundamentally our own.

32. See, e.g., Schüssler Fiorenza, *In Memory of Her*, passim.

33. As the authors have emphasized in Felder, *Stony the Road We Trod*, 6–7.

Bibliography

Aletti, Jean-Noël, S.J. *L'art de raconter Jésus Christ: L'écriture narrative de l'évangile de Luc*. Parole de Dieu. Paris: Seuil, 1989.

Anderson, Janice Capel. "Double and Triple Stories, the Implied Reader, and Redundancy in Matthew." Pp. 71–89 in *Reader Response Approaches to Biblical and Secular Texts. Semeia 31*. Robert Detweiler, ed. Atlanta: Scholars Press, 1985.

Anderson, Janice Capel, and Stephen D. Moore. *Mark and Method: New Approaches in Biblical Studies*. Minneapolis: Fortress Press, 1992.

Appiah, Kwame Anthony. *In My Father's House: Africa in the Philosophy of Culture*. New York and Oxford: Oxford University Press, 1992.

Arnett, Jill. "Feminism, Post-Structuralism and the Third World: An Assessment of Some Aspects of the Work of Gayatri Spivak." Unpublished paper, Critical Studies Group, University of Natal at Pietermaritzburg, South Africa.

Bal, Mieke. *Narratology: Introduction to the Theory of Narrative*. Trans. C. van Boemen. Toronto and Buffalo: University of Toronto Press, 1985.

———. *Femmes imaginaires. L'Ancien Testament au risque d'une narratologie critique*. Paris: Nizet, 1986.

———. *Lethal Love: Feminist Literary Readings of Biblical Love Stories*. Bloomington: Indiana University Press, 1987.

———. *Death and Dissymmetry: The Politics of Coherence in the Book of Judges*. Chicago and London: University of Chicago Press, 1988.

———. *Murder and Difference: Gender, Genre, and Scholarship on Sisera's Death*. Trans. M. Gumpert. Bloomington: Indiana University Press, 1988.

Barr, James. *Fundamentalism*. Philadelphia: Westminster Press, 1978.

———. *The Scope and Authority of the Bible*. Philadelphia: Westminster Press, 1980.

———. *Biblical Faith and Natural Theology: The Gifford Lectures for 1991*. Oxford: Clarendon Press, 1993.

Betz, Hans Dieter. *Essays on the Sermon on the Mount*. Trans. L. L. Welborn. Philadelphia: Fortress Press, 1985.

———. *Synoptische Studien II*. Tübingen: J.C.B. Mohr, 1992.

Birch, Bruce and Larry Rasmussen. *Bible and Ethics in the Christian Life*. Minneapolis: Ausburg, 1976.

Booth, Wayne C. *Critical Understanding: The Powers and Limits of Pluralism*. Chicago: University of Chicago Press, 1979.

———. *The Company We Keep: An Ethics of Fiction*. Berkeley: University of California Press, 1988.

Brown, Raymond E., S.S. *The Birth of the Messiah: A Commentary on the Infancy Narratives in Matthew and Luke*. Garden City, N.Y.: Doubleday, 1977.

Bornkamm, Günther; Gerhard Barth; Heinz Joachim Held. *Tradition and Interpretation in Matthew*. Philadelphia: Westminster Press, 1963.

Bultmann, Rudolph. *Existence and Faith: Shorter Writings of Rudolph Bultmann*. Trans. and ed. S. Ogden. Cleveland: World Publishing Company, 1960.

Burnett, Fred W. "Prolegomenon to Reading Matthew's Eschatological Discourse: Redundancy and the Education of the Reader in Matthew." Pp. 91–109 in *Reader Response Approaches to Biblical and Secular Texts. Semeia 31*. Robert Detweiler, ed. Atlanta: Scholars Press, 1985.

———. "Postmodern Biblical Exegesis: The Eve of Historical Criticism." Pp. 51–80 in *Poststructural Criticism and the Bible: Text/History/Discourse. Semeia 51*. Gary Phillips, ed. Atlanta: Scholars Press, 1990.

———. "The Undecidability of the Proper Name 'Jesus' in Matthew." Pp. 123–44 in *Poststructuralism as Exegesis. Semeia 54*. David Jobling and Stephen D. Moore, eds. Atlanta: Scholars Press, 1992.

———. "Exposing the Anti-Jewish Ideology of Matthew's Implied Author: The Characterization of God as Father." Pp. 155–91 in *Ideological Criticism of Biblical Texts. Semeia 59*. David Jobling and Tina Pippin, eds. Atlanta: Scholars Press, 1993.

Camp, Claudia V., and Carole R. Fontaine, eds. *Women, War and Metaphor. Semeia 61*. Atlanta: Scholars Press, 1993.

Cargal, Timothy B. "'His Blood Be upon Us and upon Our Children': A Matthean Double Entendre?" *NTS* 37(1991):101–12.

———. *Restoring the Diaspora: Discursive Structure and Purpose in the*

Epistle of James. SBL Dissertation Series 144. Atlanta: Scholars Press, 1993.

de Certeau, Michel. *Croire: une pratique de la différence.* Documents de travail et prépublications. Urbino: Centro Internazionale di Semiotica e di Linguistica, 1981.

———. *Heterologies: Discourse on the Other.* Trans. B. Massumi. Minneapolis: University of Minnesota Press, 1986.

Charlesworth, M. J., trans. *St. Anselm's Proslogion.* Notre Dame and London: University of Notre Dame Press, 1979.

Clayton, Jay. *The Pleasures of Babel: Contemporary American Literature and Theory.* New York and Oxford: Oxford University Press, 1993.

Coleman, Richard J. *Issues of Theological Warfare: Evangelicals and Liberals.* Grand Rapids: Wm. B. Eerdmans Publishing Co., 1972.

Collins, Adela Yarbro, ed. *Feminist Perspectives on Biblical Scholarship.* Atlanta: Scholars Press, 1985.

Cook, Michael J. "Confronting New Testament Attitudes on Jews and Judaism: Four Jewish Perspectives," in *The Chicago Theological Seminary Register,* vol. 77, no. 1 (1988).

Croatto, J. Severino. *Biblical Hermeneutics: Toward a Theory of Reading as the Production of Meaning.* Maryknoll, N.Y.: Orbis Books, 1987.

Crossan, John Dominic. *Cliffs of Fall: Paradox and Polyvalence in the Parables of Jesus.* New York: Seabury Press, 1980.

Darr, John A. *On Character Building: The Reader and the Rhetoric of Characterization in Luke-Acts.* Literary Currents in Biblical Interpretation. Louisville, Ky.: Westminster/John Knox Press, 1992.

Davies, W. D. *The Setting of the Sermon on the Mount.* Cambridge: Cambridge University Press, 1964.

Davies, W. D., and D. C. Allison, Jr. *A Critical and Exegetical Commentary on the Gospel according to Saint Matthew,* International Critical Commentaries, vols. 1 and 2. Edinburgh: T. & T. Clark, 1988, 1991.

Day, Peggy L., ed. *Gender and Difference in Ancient Israel.* Minneapolis: Fortress Press, 1989.

Delorme, Jean. *Au risque de la parole: Lire les évangiles.* Parole de Dieu. Paris: Seuil, 1991.

Detweiler, Robert, ed. *Reader Response Approaches to Biblical and Secular Texts. Semeia 31.* Atlanta: Scholars Press, 1985.

Dewey, Joanna. *Markan Public Debate: Literary Technique, Concentric Structure, and Theology in Mk. 2:1–3:6.* SBL Dissertation Series 48. Missoula, Mont.: Scholars Press, 1979.

Donaldson, Laura E. *Decolonizing Feminisms: Race, Gender, and Empire-Building.* Chapel Hill and London: University of North Carolina Press, 1992.

Dussel, Enrique. *Philosophy of Liberation*. Trans. A. Martinez and C. Morkovsky. Maryknoll, N.Y.: Orbis Books, 1985.

Eco, Umberto. *A Theory of Semiotics*. Bloomington: Indiana University Press, 1978.
———. *The Role of the Reader*. Bloomington: Indiana University Press, 1979.
Edwards, Richard A. *Matthew's Story of Jesus*. Philadelphia: Fortress Press, 1985.
———. "Uncertain Faith: Matthew's Portrait of the Disciples," in *Discipleship in the New Testament*, Fernando F. Segovia, ed. Philadelphia: Fortress Press, 1985.
Elull, J. *The Technological Society*. New York: Vintage Books, 1967.
Exum, J. Cheryl, and Johanna W. H. Bos, eds. *Reasoning with the Foxes: Female Wit in a World of Male Power. Semeia 42*. Atlanta: Scholars Press, 1988.

Farley, Edward *The Fragility of Knowledge: Theological Education in the Church and the University*. Philadelphia: Fortress Press, 1988.
Felder, Cain Hope. *Troubling Biblical Water: Race, Class, and Family*. Maryknoll, N.Y.: Orbis Books, 1989.
———, ed. *Stony the Road We Trod: African American Biblical Interpretation*. Minneapolis: Fortress Press, 1991.
Fish, Stanley. *Is There a Text in This Class?: The Authority of Interpretive Communities*. Cambridge: Harvard University Press, 1980.
Fisher, David H. "Self in Text, Text in Self." Pp. 137–54 in *Poststructural Criticism and the Bible: Text/History/Discourse. Semeia 51*. Gary Phillips, ed. Atlanta: Scholars Press, 1990.
Flashing, Darrell J. *The Ethical Challenge of Auschwitz and Hiroshima: Apocalypse or Utopia?* Albany: State University of New York Press, 1993.
Fowler, Robert M. "Who Is 'the Reader' in Reader Response Criticism?" Pp. 5–23 in *Reader Response Approaches to Biblical and Secular Texts. Semeia 31*. Robert Detweiler, ed. Atlanta: Scholars Press, 1985.
———. *Let the Reader Understand: Reader-Response Criticism and the Gospel of Mark*. Minneapolis: Fortress Press, 1991.

Gadamer, Hans-Georg. *Truth and Method*. Trans. G. Barden and J. Cumming. New York: Seabury Press, 1975.
Gueuret, Agnès. *L'engendrement d'un récit: L'évangile de l'enfance selon saint Luc*. Paris: Cerf, 1983.
Gottwald, Norman K. *The Tribes of Yahweh: A Sociology of the Religion of Liberated Israel, 1250–1050 B.C.E.* Maryknoll, N.Y.: Orbis Books, 1979.

Gottwald, Norman K., and Richard A. Horsley, eds. *The Bible and Liberation: Political and Social Hermeneutics.* Revised Edition. Maryknoll, N.Y.: Orbis Books, 1993.

Grant, Robert M., and David Tracy. *A Short History of the Interpretation of the Bible.* Philadelphia: Fortress Press, 1984.

Greimas, A. J., and J. Courtés. *Semiotics and Language: An Analytical Dictionary.* Trans. L. Crist, D. Patte, et al. Bloomington: Indiana University Press, 1982.

Haas, Peter. *Morality after Auschwitz: The Radical Challenge of the Nazi Ethic.* Philadelphia: Fortress Press, 1988.

Hallie, Philip P. *Lest Innocent Blood Be Shed: The Story of the Village of Le Chambon and How Goodness Happened There.* New York: Harper & Row, 1979.

Hamerton-Kelly, Robert G. *Sacred Violence: Paul's Hermeneutic of the Cross.* Minneapolis: Fortress Press, 1992.

Habermas, Jürgen. *Knowledge and Human Interest.* Trans. J. J. Shapiro. Boston: Beacon Press, 1971.

Harvey, Van. *The Historian and the Believer: A Confrontation between the Modern Historian's Principles of Judgment and the Christian's Will-to-Believe.* New York: Macmillan Co., 1966.

Hauerwas, Stanley. *Character and the Christian Life: A Study in Theological Ethics.* San Antonio: Trinity University Press, 1975.

———. *A Community of Character: Toward a Constructive Christian Social Ethics.* Notre Dame and London: University Of Notre Dame Press, 1981.

Heidegger, Martin. *Being and Time.* Trans. J. Macquarrie and E. Robinson. London: SCM Press, 1962.

Hesselgrave, David J., and Edward Rommen. *Contextualization: Meanings, Methods, and Models.* Leicester, England: Apollos, 1989.

Jobling, David. "Writing the Wrongs of the World: The Deconstruction of the Biblical Text in the Context of Liberation Theologies." Pp. 81–118 in *Poststructural Criticism and the Bible: Text/History/Discourse. Semeia 51.* Gary Phillips, ed. Atlanta: Scholars Press, 1990.

Jobling, David, Peggy L. Day, and Gerald T. Sheppard, eds. *The Bible and the Politics of Exegesis: Essays in Honor of Norman K. Gottwald on his Sixty-fifth Birthday.* Cleveland: Pilgrim Press, 1991.

Jobling, David, and Stephen D. Moore, eds. *Poststructuralism as Exegesis. Semeia 54.* Atlanta: Scholars Press, 1992.

Jobling, David, and Tina Pippin, eds. *Ideological Criticism of Biblical Texts. Semeia 59.* Atlanta: Scholars Press, 1993.

Johnston, Robert K. *Evangelicals at an Impasse: Biblical Authority in Practice*. Atlanta: John Knox Press, 1979.

The Kairos Document: Challenge to the Church with an introduction by J. W. de Gruchy. Grand Rapids: Wm. B. Eerdmans Publishing Co., 1986.

Kant, Immanuel. *Fundamental Principles of the Metaphysics of Morals*. New York: Bobbs-Merrill Co., 1949.

Karamaga, André. *L'Evangile en Afrique: Ruptures et continuité*. Archives vivantes. Yens/Morges: Cabédita, 1990.

Keen, Sam. *Fire in the Belly: On Being a Man*. New York: Bantam Books, 1991.

Kelber, Werner H. *The Oral and the Written Gospel: The Hermeneutics of Speaking and Writing in the Synoptic Tradition, Mark, Paul, and Q*. Philadelphia: Fortress Press, 1983.

Kingsbury, Jack D. "The Verb *Akolouthein* ('to Follow') as an Index of Matthew's View of His Community," *Journal of Biblical Literature* 97(1978):56–73.

———. *Matthew as Story*. Philadelphia: Fortress Press, 1986.

Koester, Helmut and James Robinson. *Trajectories through Early Christianity*. Philadelphia: Fortress Press, 1971.

Kuhn, Thomas. *The Structure of Scientific Revolutions*, 2d edition. Chicago and London: University of Chicago Press, 1970.

Lategan, Bernard C., and Willem S. Vorster. *Text and Reality: Aspects of Reference in Biblical Text*, Semeia Studies. Philadelphia: Fortress Press; Atlanta: Scholars Press, 1985.

Levine, Amy-Jill. *The Social and Ethnic Dimension of Matthean Salvation History*. Lewiston, N.Y.: Edwin Mellen Press, 1988.

———. "Matthew," in *The Women's Bible Commentary*, Carol A. Newsom and Sharon H. Ringe, eds. Louisville, Ky.: Westminster/John Knox Press; London: SPCK, 1992.

Lévinas, Emmanuel. *Totality and Infinity: An Essay on Exteriority*. Trans. A. Lingis. Pittsburgh: Duquesne University Press, 1969.

———. *Otherwise Than Being or Beyond Essence*. Trans. A. Lingis. The Hague: Martinus Nijhoff, 1981.

———. "De l'éthique à l'exégèse." *Les Nouveaux Cahiers* (1985)82.

———. *Ethics and Infinity*. Trans. R. Cohen. Pittsburgh: Duquesne University Press, 1985.

———. *Time and the Other*. Trans. R. Cohen. Pittsburgh: Duquesne University Press, 1987.

Luz, Ulrich. "The Disciples in the Gospel according to Matthew." Pp. 98–128 in *The Interpretation of Matthew*, G. Stanton, ed. Philadelphia: Fortress Press; London: SPCK, 1983.

————. *Matthew 1–7: A Commentary*. Minneapolis: Augsburg, 1989.

Lyons, David. *The Forms and Limits of Utilitarianism*. New York and London: Oxford University Press, 1965.

Malbon, Elizabeth Struthers. *Narrative Space and Mythic Meaning in Mark*. New Voices in Biblical Studies. San Francisco: Harper & Row, 1986.

Malina, Bruce J., and Richard L. Rohrbaugh. *Social-Science Commentary on the Synoptic Gospels*. Minneapolis: Fortress Press, 1992.

Marcel, Gabriel. *The Mystery of Being*, 2 vols. Chicago: Henry Regnery, 1950.

————. *The Existential Background of Human Dignity*. Cambridge: Harvard University Press, 1963.

Martin, Clarice. "The *Haustafeln* (Household Codes) in African American Biblical Interpretation: 'Free Slaves' and 'Subordinate Women.'" Pp. 206–31 in *Stony the Road We Trod: African American Biblical Interpretation*, Cain Hope Felder, ed. Minneapolis: Fortress Press, 1989.

Marxsen, Willi. *Mark the Evangelist: Studies on the Redaction History of the Gospel*. Nashville: Abingdon Press, 1969.

McKnight, Edgar V. *The Bible and the Reader: An Introduction to Literary Criticism*. Philadelphia: Fortress Press, 1985.

Miller, David. "The Question of the Book: Religion as Texture." Pp. 53–64 in *Text and Textuality. Semeia 40*. Charles E. Winquist, ed. Atlanta: Scholars Press, 1987.

Moore, Stephen. *Literary Criticism and the Gospels: The Theoretical Challenge*. New Haven: Yale University Press, 1989.

Mosala, Itumeleng J. *Biblical Hermeneutics and Black Theology in South Africa*. Grand Rapids: Wm. B. Eerdmans Publishing Co., 1989.

Myers, Ched. *Binding the Strong Man: A Political Reading of Mark's Story of Jesus*. Maryknoll, N.Y.: Orbis Books, 1988.

Newsom, Carol A., and Sharon H. Ringe, eds. *The Women's Bible Commentary*. Louisville, Ky.: Westminster/John Knox Press; London: SPCK, 1992.

Nolan, Albert. *Jesus Before Christianity*. 2d ed. Cape Town: David Philip Publisher, 1976

————. *God in South Africa: The Challenge of the Gospel*. Cape Town: David Philip Publisher; Grand Rapids: Wm. B. Eerdmans Publishing Co., 1988.

Nolan, Albert, and Richard Broderick. *To Nourish Our Faith: Theology of Liberation for South Africa*. Hilton, South Africa: Cornerstone Books, 1987.

Odell-Scott, David. *A Post-Patriarchal Christology*. American Academy of Religion Series. Atlanta: Scholars Press, 1992.

Ogletree, Thomas W. *The Use of the Bible in Christian Ethics*. Philadelphia: Fortress Press, 1983.

Panier, Louis. *La naissance du fils de Dieu: Sémiotique et théologie discursive. Lecture de Luc 1–2*. Théologie et Sciences Religieuses *Cogitatio fidei*. Paris: Cerf, 1991.

Paris, Peter J. "The Bible and the Black Churches." Pp. 133–54 in *The Bible and Social Reform*. The Bible in American Culture. Ernest R. Sandeen, ed. Philadelphia: Fortress Press and Chico, Calif.: Scholars Press, 1982.

———. *The Social Teaching of the Black Churches*. Philadelphia: Fortress Press, 1985.

Patte, Daniel. *L'Athéisme d'un Chrétien ou un Chrétien à l'écoute de Sartre*. Paris: Nouvelles Editions Latines, 1965.

———. *What Is Structural Exegesis?* Philadelphia: Fortress Press, 1976.

———. *Paul's Faith and the Power of the Gospel: A Structural Introduction to Paul's Letters*. Philadelphia: Fortress Press, 1983.

———. *The Gospel according to Matthew: A Structural Commentary on Matthew's Faith*. Philadelphia: Fortress Press, 1987.

———. "Anti-Semitism in the New Testament: Confronting the Dark Side of Paul's and Matthew's Teaching." In "The New Testament and Judaica/Judaism," *Chicago Theological Seminary Register*, vol. 78, no. 1 (1988):31–52.

———. "Bringing Out of the Gospel-Treasure What Is New and What Is Old: Two Parables in Matthew 18–23," *Quarterly Review* vol. 10, no. 3 (1990): 79–108

———. *Religious Dimensions of Biblical Texts: Greimas's Structural Semiotics and Biblical Exegesis*. SBL Semeia Studies. Atlanta: Scholars Press, 1990.

———. *Structural Exegesis for New Testament Critics*. Minneapolis: Fortress Press, 1990.

———. "Textual Constraints, Ordinary Readings, and Critical Exegeses: An Androcritical Perspective." Pp. 59–79 in *Textual Determinacy: Part One. Semeia 62*. Robert C. Culley and Robert B. Robinson, eds. Atlanta: Scholars Press, 1993.

———. *Discipleship according to the Sermon on the Mount: A Multidimensional Androcritical Exegesis*. (forthcoming).

Patte, Daniel, and Gary Phillips. "A Fundamental Condition for Ethical Accountability in the Teaching of the Bible by White Male Exegetes: Recovering and Claiming the Specificity of Our Perspective." *Scriptura: Journal of Bible and Theology in Southern Africa.* Special Issue S9(1992):7–28.

———. *Teaching the Bible Otherwise: Can We Be Responsible and Critical in a Pluralistic Context?* (forthcoming).

Perrin, Norman. *Jesus and the Language of the Kingdom.* Philadelphia: Fortress Press, 1976.

Petitot, Jean. *Les catastrophes de la parole: de R. Jakobson à R. Thom.* Paris: Maloine, 1985.

Phillips, Gary A. "History and Text: The Reader in Context in Matthew's Parables Discourse." Pp. 111–38 in *Reader Response Approaches to Biblical and Secular Texts. Semeia 31.* Robert Detweiler, ed. Atlanta: Scholars Press, 1985.

———. "Exegesis as Critical Praxis: Reclaiming History and Text from a Postmodern Perspective." Pp. 7–49 in *Poststructural Criticism. Semeia 51.* Atlanta: Scholars Press, 1990.

———. "Sign/Text/Différance: The Contribution of Intertextual Theory to Biblical Criticism." Pp. 78–101 in *Intertextuality,* H. Plett, ed. Untersuchungen zu Texttheorie 15. Berlin: de Gruyter, 1991.

Phillips, Gary A., ed. *Poststructural Criticism and the Bible: Text/History/ Discourse. Semeia 51.* Atlanta: Scholars Press, 1990.

Plank, Karl A. *Paul and the Irony of Affliction.* Semeia Studies. Atlanta: Scholars Press, 1987.

Ricoeur, Paul. *The Conflict of Interpretations: Essays in Hermeneutics.* Evanston, Ill.: Northwestern University Press, 1974.

———. "Qu'est-ce qu'un texte? Expliquer et comprendre." Pp. 181–200 in *Hermeneutik und Dialektik, Aufsätze II: Hans-Georg Gadamer zum 70. Geburtstag,* Rudiger Bubner, Konrad Cramer, and Reiner Wiehl, eds. Tübingen: J.C.B. Mohr, 1970.

———. *Hermeneutics and the Human Sciences.* Trans. J. B. Thompson. Cambridge: Cambridge University Press, 1981.

———. *Oneself as Another.* Trans. K. Blamey. Chicago and London: University of Chicago Press, 1992.

The Road to Damascus: Kairos and Conversion. London: CIIR; Washington: Center of Concern; London: Christian Aid, 1989.

Robbins, Vernon K. *Jesus the Teacher: A Socio-Rhetorical Interpretation of Mark.* Philadelphia: Fortress Press, 1984.

Rowland, Christopher, and Mark Corner. *Liberating Exegesis: The Challenge of Liberation Theology to Biblical Studies.* Louisville, Ky.: Westminster/John Knox Press, 1989.

Russell, Letty M., ed. *Feminist Interpretation of the Bible.* Philadelphia: Westminster Press, 1985.

Said, Edward W. *Orientalism*. New York: Pantheon, 1978.

———. *The World, the Text, and the Critic*. Cambridge: Harvard University Press, 1983.

———. *Culture and Imperialism*. New York: Alfred A. Knopf, 1994.

Sandmel, Samuel. *Anti-Semitism in the New Testament?* Philadelphia: Fortress Press, 1978.

Schaberg, Jane. *The Illegitimacy of Jesus*. New York: Crossroad, 1990.

———. "Luke." In *The Women's Bible Commentary*, Carol A. Newsom and Sharon H. Ringe, eds. Louisville, Ky.: Westminster/John Knox Press; London: SPCK, 1992.

Scharlemann, Robert P. "Theological text." Pp. 5–19 in *Text and Textuality. Semeia 40*. Charles E. Winquist, ed. Atlanta: Scholars Press, 1987.

Schottroff, Willy, and Wolfgang Stegemann, eds. *God of the Lowly: Socio-Historical Interpretations of the Bible*. Trans. M. J. O'Connell. Maryknoll, N.Y.: Orbis Books, 1984.

Schubeck, Thomas L., S.J. *Liberation Ethics: Sources, Models, and Norms*. Minneapolis: Fortress Press, 1993.

Schüssler Fiorenza, Elisabeth. *In Memory of Her: A Feminist Theological Reconstruction of Christian Origins*. New York: Crossroad, 1983.

———. *Bread Not Stone: The Challenge of Feminist Biblical Interpretation*. Boston: Beacon Press, 1984.

———. "The Ethics of Interpretation: De-Centering Biblical Scholarship." *Journal of Biblical Literature*, 107(1988):3–17.

———. *Revelation: Vision of a Just World*. Minneapolis: Fortress Press, 1991.

———. *But She Said: Feminist Practices of Biblical Interpretation*. Boston: Beacon Press, 1992.

———. *Discipleship of Equals: A Critical Feminist Ekklesia-logy of Liberation*. New York: Crossroad, 1993.

Schwartz, Regina M. "Joseph's Bones and the Resurrection of the Text: Remembering in the Bible." Pp. 40–59 in *The Book and the Text: The Bible and Literary Theory*. Oxford and Cambridge, Mass.: Blackwell, 1990.

Schwartz, Regina M., ed. *The Book and the Text: The Bible and Literary Theory*. Oxford and Cambridge, Mass.: Blackwell, 1990.

Schweitzer, Albert. *The Quest of the Historical Jesus: A Critical Study of Its Progress from Reimarus to Wrede*, with an introduction by James Robinson. New York: Macmillan Co., 1968.

Schweizer, Eduard. *The Good News according to Matthew*. Atlanta: John Knox Press, 1975.

Scott, Bernard Brandon. *Hear Then the Parable: A Commentary on the Parables of Jesus*. Philadelphia: Fortress Press, 1989.

Smart, James. *The Strange Silence of the Bible in the Church*. Philadelphia: Westminster Press, 1970.

Spivak, Gayatri Chakravorty. "Scattered Speculations on the Question of Value." *Diacritics* 15(1985):73–93.

———. "Can the Subaltern Speak?" Pp. 277–313 in *Marxism and the Interpretation of Culture*, G. Nelson and L. Grossberg, eds. London: Macmillan Publishers, 1988.

———. *In Other Worlds*. New York: Methuen, 1987.

Standaert, Benoit. *L'Evangile de Marc: Composition et Genre Littéraire*. Brugge: Zevenkerken, 1978.

Stanton, Graham. "The Origin and Purpose of Matthew's Gospel: Matthean Scholarship from 1945 to 1980." Pp. 1889–1951 in *Aufstieg und Niedergang der Römischen Welt* II.25.3. H. Temporini and W. Haase, eds. Berlin: Walter de Gruyter, 1983.

Stendahl, Krister. "Biblical Theology, Contemporary," Pp. 418–32 in *The Interpreter's Dictionary of the Bible*, vol 1. Nashville, Abingdon Press, 1962.

Sternberg, Meir. *The Poetics of Biblical Narrative: Ideological Literature and the Drama of Reading*. Bloomington: Indiana University Press, 1987.

Stout, Jeffrey. *Ethics after Babel: The Languages of Morals and Their Discontents*. Boston: Beacon Press, 1988.

Strecker, Georg. *Der Weg der Gerechtigkeit: Untersuchung zur Theologie des Matthaus*. Gottingen: Vandenhoeck and Ruprecht, 1962.

———. "The Concept of History in Matthew." Pp. 67–84 in *The Interpretation of Matthew*, G. Stanton, ed. Philadelphia: Fortress Press; London: SPCK, 1983.

———. *The Sermon on the Mount: An Exegetical Commentary*. Trans. O. C. Dean, Jr. Nashville: Abingdon Press, 1988.

Sugirtharajah, R. S., ed. *Voices from the Margin: Interpreting the Bible in the Third World*. Maryknoll, N.Y.: Orbis Books, 1991.

Tannehill, Robert C. *The Narrative Unity of Luke-Acts: A Literary Interpretation*. Volume 1: *The Gospel according to Luke*. Foundations and Facets: New Testament. Philadelphia: Fortress Press, 1986.

Thom, René. *Modèles mathématiques de la morphogenèse*. Paris: Bourgeois, 1980.

———. *Paraboles et catastrophes*. Paris: Flammarion, 1983.

Van Tilborg, Sjef. *The Sermon on the Mount as an Ideological Intervention: A Reconstruction of Meaning*. Assen/Maastricht: Van Gorcum, 1986.

Tillich, Paul. *The Dynamics of Faith*. New York: Harper and Brothers, 1957.

Tolbert, Mary Ann. *Perspectives on the Parables: An Approach to Multiple Interpretations*. Philadelphia: Fortress Press, 1979.

————. *Sowing the Gospel: Mark's World in Literary-Historical Perspective*, Minneapolis: Fortress Press, 1989.

Tolbert, Mary Ann, ed. *The Bible and Feminist Hermeneutics. Semeia 28.* Atlanta: Scholars Press, 1983.

Tracy, David. "Interpretation of the Bible and Interpretation Theory." Pp. 153–66 in Robert M. Grant and David Tracy, *A Short History of the Interpretation of the Bible*. Philadelphia: Fortress Press, 1984.

Trible, Phyllis. *God and the Rhetoric of Sexuality*. Philadelphia: Fortress Press, 1978.

Troeltsch, Ernst. "Historiography." Pp. 716–23 in *Encyclopedia of Religion and Ethics*, vol. 6, James Hastings, ed. New York: Charles Scribner's Sons, 1914.

————. *Religion in History: Essays*. Trans. J. L. Adams and Walter F. Bense. Fortress Texts in Modern Theology. Minneapolis: Fortress Press, 1991.

Vahanian, Gabriel. *Dieu anonyme ou la peur des mots*. Paris: Desclée de Brouwer, 1989.

————. *L'utopie chrétienne*. Paris: Desclée de Brouwer, 1992.

Via, Dan O., Jr. *The Ethics of Mark's Gospel in the Middle of Time*. Philadelphia: Fortress Press, 1985.

————. *Self-Deception and Wholeness in Paul and Matthew*. Minneapolis: Fortress Press, 1990.

Violence, The New Kairos: Challenges to the Churches. Johannesburg: Institute for Contextual Theology, 1990.

Weems, Renita J. *Just a Sister Away: A Womanist Vision of Women's Relationships in the Bible*. San Diego, Calif.: LuraMedia, 1988.

————. "Reading *Her Way* through the Struggle: African American Women and the Bible," in *Stony the Road We Trod: African American Biblical Interpretation*, Cain H. Felder, ed. Minneapolis: Fortress Press,1991.

————. *Marriage, Sex, and Violence: Hebrew Rhetoric and Audience*. Minneapolis: Fortress Press, 1992.

Welch, Sharon D. *Communities of Resistance and Solidarity: A Feminist Theology of Liberation*. Maryknoll, N.Y.: Orbis Books, 1985.

————. *A Feminist Ethic of Risk*. Minneapolis: Fortress Press, 1990.

West, Cornel. "Ethics and Actions in Frederic Jameson's Marxist Hermeneutics." Pp. 123–44 in *Postmodernism and Politics*, Jonathan Arac, ed. Theory and Literary History 28. Minneapolis: University of Minnesota Press, 1985.

West, Gerald. *Biblical Hermeneutics of Liberation: Modes of Reading the Bible in the South African Context.* Pietermaritzburg, South Africa: Cluster Publications, 1991.

————. *Contextual Bible Study.* Pietermaritzburg, South Africa: Cluster Publications, 1993.

Wink, Walter. *The Bible in Human Transformation: Toward a New Paradigm for Biblical Study.* Philadelphia: Fortress Press, 1973.

Zumstein, Jean. *La condition du croyant dans l'Evangile selon Matthieu.* Göttingen: Vandenhoeck and Ruprecht, 1977.